THE
ACCIDENTAL
BUS
DRIVER

by Thomas Beaumont

Vacker Berg

For more information on the Accidental Bus Driver go to
www.accidentalbusdriver.com

© Thomas Beaumont 2014

ISBN 978-0-9927612-0-2

Published in 2014 by Vacker Berg Böcker

E-mail: accidentbusdriver@btinternet.com

Cover designed by Alice Feaver.

Photographs by Thomas Beaumont.

Design & Production: Trevor Preece – trevor@trpub.net

Printed by: Ashford Colour Press Ltd, Gosport, Hampshire

CONTENTS

CHAPTER 9

Welcome Back:
Snow, Yorkshire Breakfasts, The Flying Pig
and Trouble in the Land that God Forgot   197

*The Accidental Bus
Driver, drawn by
Malky McCormick*

PREFACE

Boris Johnson and I went to school together. I don't remember much about him, except for his blonde mop which was readily identifiable. He was younger and far cleverer than me and in a school the size of Eton, it was unlikely that a King's Scholar with a future eye on politics and myself, who wanted only to head for the nearest betting shop, pub, nightclub or racecourse, would ever have much in common. But as life is full of surprises, amazingly we do.

In later life, we both find ourselves involved in buses. Boris, of course in a more prominent role than myself, being active in Transport for London, taking a bus to the Beijing Olympics in 2008 to promote London 2012 and being instrumental in designing a new Routemaster, ensuring the return of the much loved double deckers to the city.

I just became a bus driver.

I am certainly not the first Old Etonian bus driver, but must be one of an elite few who have followed this career path. My contemporaries are captains of industry, Q.C's, chairmen of banks, successful hedge funders, members of the cabinet, headmasters, vicars, owners of a successful fashion business and all kinds of other interesting professions. And that wasn't a particularly vintage year. There were no Prime Ministers, Archbishops of Canterbury, Olympic medallists, actors, comedians, newspaper editors or game show hosts.

So have I underachieved?

On the face of it I might have done. I have had many careers in my life – worked for a bookmaker, sold badges made out of scrapped nuclear weapons for a charity, worked on Wogan's Winner on Radio 2, driven trucks to communist Poland, worked in the express courier industry, fashion world, government statistics, stable lad, tour guide, builder's mate and biscuit maker.

A bus driver was just another move in my eccentrically diverse life. Though I may have accidentally gone into the industry, I've never regretted it due to the continuing rich mixture of unconventional characters and situations which gives hours of pleasure to someone such as myself who counts one of his pleasures as being an observer of life.

Hence I wanted to write my experiences down. They are a record of what life was like on the buses at the end of the 20th and into the early 21st centuries. I wanted it to show the depth in the bus industry and the camaraderie of those who work within it. It is a tough world and bus drivers deserve to be acknowledged for their efforts, toughness and sense of humour.

I have not used the real names of most places and individuals, in case I caused any unintended hurt. That is the last thing I intended to do and there are many people I would like to thank for their kindness and tolerance towards me. They have been long suffering. They will know who they are.

I hope you enjoy reading of things which have happened to me.

Oh, and one last thing. You may be wondering about the word 'Accidental' in the title of this book. I have already said that I fell into the career by accident, but I neglected to mention that in my volatile life I have been in 17 car crashes, a tractor smash, 7 near misses on planes, a train hitting the buffers, a tube train when all the doors flew open when it was accelerating out of a station and even a head-on narrow boat collision on the Regent's Park Canal. This will whet your appetite and give a hint of what happened to me in the world of buses. Then you will be able to decide whether the double entendre of the title, The Accidental Bus Driver is justified.

Fasten your seat belts and please read on.

THOMAS BEAUMONT, March 2014

Welcome to the eloquent world of buses. This is a typical example of what you find when the children have disembarked the school bus.

Heavy going in Ilocos Norte Province in the Philippines as London Express is bogged down again.

Travelling in North West China was like going back in time as each morning the owner driver started the bus by hand.

The Jeepney, London
Express has to be dug
out of the soft sands on
a day drip to the
mountains.

Comfort may not have
been the top priority with
most buses I jumped on in
downtown Yangon.

Stuck for the third time the same day. This time involved an unscheduled dip in the middle of a fast flowing river.

Speeding along the rough roads somewhere in Gansu, China, a bus heads for the capital Lanzhou.

Chapter 1

CHAPTER ONE

THE LONG & ACCIDENTAL ROAD TO BECOMING A BUS DRIVER

The sparrow shat on my shoulder at 9.13am precisely.

The Gent electrical clock, situated above the main door of the building, stated this. It was a dour clock in a dour building. The building was made out of bricks and steel girders with large and austere window frames set at regular intervals along the side. Most of the glass panes were broken; some were without glass altogether, blown out by the unforgiving northerly wind, though a few had clung on to their putty and, therefore were fine examples of early continental Edwardian craftsmanship. Architecturally speaking, the building was a close relative of the Soviet tractor factory at Stalingrad.

The time was always 9.13. The Gent clock had not worked for many years. It had short circuited, in a display of spitting and crackling, while sparks rained down on the scattering huddle of bus drivers twenty five feet below, before giving up the ghost. No attempt had been made to replace or repair the sad looking clock. One reason perhaps was because of the precarious state of the ladders kept in the depot which would be needed for carrying out this task and were deemed far too dangerous for any form of climbing. The last time one of the mechanics had tried to change a light bulb in the roof, the rungs had cracked and he came back down to earth with a bump.

The sparrow actually shat on my shoulder at around 4.30am. It was surprising that so many sparrows were up so early in the morning, performing the dawn chorus and exercising their bowel muscles. It was not light yet. Somewhere in the gloom, I tripped over the watering can I had been looking for, half-full with the pre-made mix of 75% water and 25% anti-freeze. I found the old, oil stained cloth when I sat down on the bench outside the office and received several oily streaks to my trouser seat, as a result of my failure to look before I sat. The white streak on my shoulder was by now turning the colour of a duck's egg, the anti-freeze mix was causing a burning sensation on a newly formed cut on my thumb and I thought I heard, amongst the chatter of the sparrows, the sound of the crucial button on my trousers giving way and bouncing on the concrete floor.

This was nothing unusual. The start to my bus driving day was always chaotic, panic stricken and disorganised, yet organised enough to arrive at the destination on time. That was just how it was.

I was off to a school in Yorkshire. It was a town that I had never been to before, which was an added pressure when not only having an early start, but also having to navigate in the dark. They had requested a bus for 8.30am to take the children and teachers to an outward bound centre in the Pennines. The twisting roads were bound to induce travel sickness and, from past experience, some of the schools from that area tended to be louder than most other schools. The teachers, too, would have voices like foghorns and there would be plenty of shouted rebukes like 'shut it – you at the back' and 'stop eating those sweets, but would you like some more chocolate?' This, of course would have the effect of making the children sicker, faster. It was with a sense of impending doom that I set off.

First light broke over the moorland tops. The relative peace and tranquillity were moments in any bus driver's day which were to be savoured for their rarity. Driving at dawn was one of those times. It was just you, nature and the elements. No passengers. No deadlines. No stress or strain. This morning the skies were icy blue. The rising orange sun was hovering over the heather clad Pennine hills.

The air was crisp. The dew laden fields and the cuckoo's spit by the side of the road began to sparkle as the sun strengthened. The sheep munched the vegetation in slow contentment, seemingly glad for some warmth on their backs. The birds were at their most cheerful, flying alongside the bus, occasionally showing off with an acrobatic manoeuvre. The towns and villages were deserted. The roads were empty.

All was well with the world.

I swept majestically round the corner to find a scene you might have found somewhere in the Balkans and not the North of England. There was a man castigating his donkey in the middle of the road, causing me to bring the bus to an abrupt halt. The man wore a trilby hat with a feather sticking out of it. The donkey had dug its toes into the tarmac. The owner tried to talk to his beast, failed and turned towards me. He shrugged his shoulders, raised his eyes skywards before returning to his donkey. He went to its rear and gave the donkey a determined kick up the backside.

The donkey shot into the air, braying frantically, before getting the message and trotting down the road, into a lay-by, which was full of gypsy caravans, horses and dark and beautiful people. The penny dropped. It was nearly Appleby Fair time. Travellers and gypsies from all over the world were converging on the small Westmorland town in the Eden Valley from all parts of the world. I was driving on one of the main arterial routes to the Horse Fair.

As I drove on, I looked in my wing mirror and watched the man hugging his donkey. They must have made up. This had to be an omen. Today was going to be a good day. And so it turned out to be. At the next T-junction, I heard a loud grating noise. A dodgy looking Toyota pick-up pulling a caravan with no tyres appeared out of the mist at top speed. The driver looked nervous. The metal hubs of the caravan were making grooves in the tarmac road and showering sparks as they went. It was obvious that they were out at this hour in an attempt to avoid any police.

I arrived at the school three hours later. It lived up to my expectations and as so often happened on my trips to Yorkshire the teacher in charge proudly announced when I arrived that the children had been given a good breakfast. Sausage, bacon, baked beans, black pudding, mushrooms, fried tomatoes, fried bread, fried egg and hash browns and a banana milkshake. For good measure the teachers were carrying a snack which consisted of chocolate digestives, Mars bars and some fizzy pop, yet they requested that we made a stop at Scotch Corner Services, in case they were still hungry.

I've never driven so slowly in my life. I was half an hour late, but it was worth every minute. Despite the teachers' shouts of 'pass the vomit bucket – quick, quick, someone's not feeling well', and the sounds of retching and moaning, not one child was sick. This was indeed a good day.

"Job's a goodun", said the boss when I returned to base.

How did I become a bus driver? It was by accident, naturally. It was not a career which readily sprang to mind or something I had a passion for when I was younger. Buses were functional, they were bland but they were always around if you needed them. As a child most of my contemporaries wanted to be train drivers or astronauts. I was more or less the same except, owing to my passion for horseracing, I wanted to be a jockey. That was never going to happen as I was always tall for my age and if family history was a guide, I was going to be well over 6ft. I prayed my gangly physique might save the day but at the age of ten the family GP quietly gave me the devastating news that I wouldn't make it as a jockey.

I never considered buses as an alternative career. A gambler or a stable lad seemed the most appealing job. My early associations with buses were, most likely, little different from the rest of the British population in the 1970s. I watched *On The Buses*, Cliff Richard driving a red London double-decker in *Summer Holiday*, Michael Caine driving a coach over the cliff in *The Italian Job*, Roger Moore demolishing the top deck by going under a low bridge in *Live And Let Die* and Clint Eastwood getting his bus shot to bits by the local police in *The Gauntlet*. Buses only lost their dowdy image and became sexy in the 1990s when Sandra Bullock took the wheel of the school bus in *Speed*.

When I look back I seem to have had idyllic memories of travelling on buses from early childhood. In the 1960s there was a queue at the bus stop opposite my Surrey school, with children waiting for the distinctive two toned green and cream Aldershot & District service buses, which seemed through a child's eyes to go to every place on earth. The drivers were very smart, they wore a suit, ironed shirt and tie, polished black shoes and sometimes a peaked cap with cap badge. Hanging off their belts was a large circular metal badge in a leather holder. They exuded politeness and confidence. They knew each and every child; their names and the stop where they would get off.

I had this grown up feeling of independence and freedom every day as I handed over my 3d bit to the driver and received a curled up roll of thin paper as a ticket in return. The bus would drop me at the end of the lane and it was a five-minute walk home. There were few rules. "Don't accept a lift from a stranger in a car and stay on the lane. Don't walk through Mr Money's wood," Mother always used to say. Life encouraged trust and travelling alone on buses as a 5-year-old was the norm.

In hindsight it was a utopian, bygone age. I was lucky enough to have been a part of this normal existence where children did not have to be mollycoddled and parents did not live in fear of paedophiles lurking round every corner.

The fond memories of buses continued during summer holidays on the beach at Westgate-on-Sea in Kent. The beautiful cream and maroon East Kent buses were unlike anything I had ever seen as they were open topped. Children would race up the stairs to the top deck to grab the front seat and feel the gentle breeze and warmth of the sun as the bus gently rolled along the seafront towards Margate. Seagulls would swoop and hover over the bus in the hope of grabbing a piece of half eaten ice cream cone. The bus ambled along the white coastal road, passing the rows of hotels and guest houses on one side of the road and the beach on the other. There were donkeys on the beach, each with a different coloured bridle with their name embroidered on the leather. Andy, Brian and Jessica walked slowly, on a lead rein, from one end of the beach to the other, close to the ramp where the pedalos were launched. On the sea wall there were two ice cream vendors, one selling Walls and the other selling Lyons Maid, though both sold the bestselling 99 ice cream cone.

The waft of creosote from the coloured changing huts mixed with sun cream and tanning oil reached the top deck. It was the picture postcard seaside resort. We drove past the sunken garden, the row of Victorian canopied shops with buckets, spades, rubber rings and windmills hanging from the walls. Then, the highlight of the journey was when the route turned away from the sea and passed a hospital for incurables or veterans or probably incurable veterans. The patients and nurses would wave at the passing bus from their beds which had been brought outside into the hospital garden.

The older I got, the less romantic buses seemed to become. They just became a means to an end. As a teenager at boarding school I would occasionally make illegal trips to the Granada Cinema in

Slough on the service bus, commonly known as the 'Ghost Bus'. Its name derived from the fact that, at night, there was a blue light in the driver's cab, which made it impossible to make out the shape or form of the driver, and it therefore appeared that there was nobody driving.

When I turned 17 and left school to travel and work my way around the world, buses were to become a necessity for in many parts of the world it was the only practical and cheap form of transport. In some cases it was positively dangerous and some journeys became near-death experiences. Most were akin to bone-rattlers and subjected the passenger to great discomfort, overcrowding, smells, heat and evidence of scant maintenance; but all of them got me there in the end.

In the 1980s, Greyhound Lines were the cheapest way to see America. The downside was having to pass through the dowdy and sometimes dangerous bus stations, which were magnets for all sorts of people. News stories of murders, rapes, hijackings and thefts were not uncommon. Depressingly, if you survived the experience you were not hailed a hero. Instead I had to suffer the galling experience of being pigeonholed as a third class citizen. I once arrived in Miami where my host was in a cold sweat when he met me at the decrepit terminus and genuinely said how glad he was to see me alive as there had been numerous recent stabbings across the country.

My first bus crash occurred in Australia and was thanks indirectly to an old school friend I inadvertently bumped into in Brisbane High Street. When I told him that I was keen to do a 'round Australia' coach tour, he recommended this alternative company based somewhere near the Gold Coast. It was so small, that it only had one bus.

Arriving at the picking up point at Brisbane Coach Station, I noticed a ragtag group of people milling around. They looked to be an assorted bunch. I started to think I would personally throttle my friend when I next saw him, for his obvious poor recommendation. This was undoubtedly the bargain basement end of coach tours and not the luxury he had talked about. Deluxe coach after deluxe coach came swooping gracefully into the coach bays, glistening with polish and smart, smiling uniformed staff appeared and whisked away the smart looking tourists. They all had the latest suitcases, whereas the queue for our coach was littered with backpacks and plastic bags.

Finally, about two hours after due departure time, there was a nerve jangling noise like a washing machine with a cracked bearing, going through its final cycle. Suddenly this vision appeared which bore little resemblance to a bus. It was a dusty, silver, cocooned structure which looked more like an American hamburger vending trailer. It drew to a halt, brakes whining, dust circulating and black smoke emanating in regular dragon-sized puffs from the exhaust. The doors tried to open but the air pressure was not great enough to do the job. This was followed by the sounds of hobnailed boots on the panel and fists banging on the glass. The doors sprung open and two figures announced: "She'll be right mate."

Similar to watching a scene from a science fiction film, the group of passengers stood and gaped with a mixture of disbelief, surprise and nervous anticipation of what was going to happen next and who was going to come down the steps? Two burly and dusty bus drivers stepped down, wearing sky blue t-shirts and alarming denim shorts made out of cut off jeans. They wore bush hats and fake designer sunglasses.

"G'day everybody, I'm Archie," said the slimmer of the two.

"And I'm Ned," joined in the squatter of the two. The elasticity of the flab around his belly which wobbled violently against the cotton t-shirt betrayed a partiality for a beer or two. Behind that there was an iron man who was as strong as an ox, as he would prove later in the trip.

"Streuth," said one of the passengers, a nurse from Sydney. "He's built like a brick shithouse." She was mentally undressing him on the bus station concourse.

So we loaded up and set off with the flabbergasted stares and sneering laughter of the public in the coach station. We hadn't gone far when one of the passengers came down to the front to complain of a smell of sewage and noticed that a trickle of unfortunately coloured liquid seemed to be flowing down the aisle. She was closely followed by one of the younger ladies and her fiancée. Tia could bear the smell no longer and was holding her Chanel atomiser above her head, liberally spraying No.5 wherever and over whomever she could. Ryan, the bespectacled fiancé was desperately trying to wrest the bottle away from her. This was never going to happen as he was a few inches shorter than her and could only just reach the top of her head.

The scene promoted a great deal of bad humour, coughing and retching. It was a thoroughly grumpy coach. It was a rotten way to begin the tour. People's confidence, which had been at a low ebb when they first saw the vintage bus, was now at rock bottom. The mixed aromas of excreta and French perfume caused a chemical reaction and noxious gases spread through the bus, which proved to be the final straw for the drivers when they reached the front of the bus.

"Oh Jesus bloody Christ," yelled Ned, braking hard, steering the bus with his elbows while crunching the gears with one hand and desperately holding his nose with the other.

The bus came to a halt just before a busy intersection. The drivers kicked the doors open and ran to the back of the bus. One of them must have pulled a lever as there was a clunking noise immediately followed by the sound of rushing water. They jumped back into the bus and drove off as fast as they could, leaving the river of blue chemically enhanced urine accompanied with floating objects on the surface, bubbling gently towards the drains next to the traffic lights. There was a policeman standing with one foot in the road, in blissful ignorance of what was happening. Even when the trickle became a river and ran between his legs, miraculously, he did not notice.

The PA system crackled, "No worries people, the toilets are now back in business and ready for use." All the tour party sat motionless in their seats. Nobody said anything to anybody. This must be a one-off problem we all thought.

We thought wrongly. Several miles further on, just as we had cleared city limits the coach stopped. After a debate the two drivers got off the bus. Ned crawled under the front of the bus and Archie handed him a bunch of tea towels. When they re-boarded they explained that this was an old bus and that the gearbox and clutch were a little indifferent and causing problems. These were easily solved by wrapping tea towels around them which would help keep them in place and working. The only down side was that they needed replacing every 80 kilometres.

"We'll have to stop every hour or so," Ned informed the passengers. "But no worries, there won't be any problems as there's a plentiful supply of tea towels."

No one complained and on we travelled. The bus was silent and all the travellers kept themselves to themselves. This turned out to be the quiet before the storm as daylight turned to dusk and around 7pm we were approaching Proserpine on the Queensland coast. We were not too far from our first night's camping stop.

I was sitting in the aisle seat directly behind the driver. Ned was driving along the coast road. As the bus went round a long, sweeping corner at between 65 to 70mph, there was a loud bang; a bang which sounded like a part of the engine exploding.

Ned blasted out a warning, "Watch out everybody! Steering's jammed. Hold on!"

Everything went into slow motion. The bus took a sharp left turn off the road and headed into the bush. It is strange how the brain works when you are faced with the feeling that the end is nigh. My initial and short lived reaction was how amusing and surreal this all was, before panic made an entrance. "This is it", I thought as I looked out of the front window and prayed that there were no large gum trees in our path that we were going to plough into. The English side of me (I am half English and half Scottish) made sure I maintained my stiff upper lip and didn't let on to the others that, like them, I was 'shitting bricks'.

The bus kept going and going. It did not seem to slow down at all. We demolished small and medium sized trees and shrubs. It lurched, rotated and pirouetted from side to side, but remained upright. Somewhere in our journey into the bush I had the uneasy feeling that the seat armrest I was gripping on to for grim life, or death, was not doing its job. When I looked down I saw that I was holding on to the armrest in mid air. It had become detached from the rest of the seat and I was holding on to a useless piece of plastic. Other passengers were staring at this piece of absolute futility with fear and amusement. It took their minds of the reality of what might be coming to us all.

No one screamed. No one made any noise at all. Amongst the sound of crashing foliage everyone kept a dignified calm, even though many later said that their lives flashed before their eyes. Did I experience the old adage of smelling fear? I'm not sure but the Chanel No. 5 seemed to linger in the air. I have never liked that smell to this day, it triggers bad memories. The feeling of blood draining from my face, being in a cold sweat and shakiness was most real. It was a feeling I had felt many times in my life; thanks to already being a veteran of numerous car crashes and accidents on other forms of transport, but this was the first time I had experienced it on a bus.

The bus began to slow and eventually came to a stop a few metres from the main Brisbane to Townsville railway line. It was silent. Slowly people came to terms with the fact that we had all had a lucky escape. I turned around and some began to smile, then giggle then laugh rumbustiously at the realisation of still being alive. Everyone cheered, leapt down the coach steps and milled around the crashed vehicle. The bus was tough and relatively untouched. There were a few dents but nothing that was not fixable.

"She'll be right by the morning," said Ned. He was true to his word.

I remember being more concerned about standing in the middle of the Queensland bush where there was a strong likelihood that a taipan or tiger snake might be lurking nearby and would, most likely, be very angry at having his siesta ruined by some dilapidated old bus. Human nature is a strange beast and the delayed shock of what we had been through did not occur until several hours later. But by then we were all too pissed to really take stock.

The ice was well and truly broken. Great friendships were made and the relief of just being alive manifested itself in singing, revelry and amazing Queensland steaks washed down with copious quantities of Hunter Valley white and Bundaberg OP (Overproof) Rum. In fact most of the wine, beer and spirit making areas of Australia were investigated and sampled that night around a camp fire.

It was Ned the coach driver who was the hero. The cause of the accident was traced to the steering, which had jammed, forcing us off the road at such a high speed. Ned's fast reactions and incredible strength managed to bend the steering rod to such a degree that the coach kept a straight line and did not flip over. His cool head saved our lives.

The next day we were on the road again, hungover but happy. The steering was mended and the supply of tea towels was replenished. All the passengers were offered a refund and a chance to go home. Not one did. These days after such a crash, there would be counsellors, health and safety, arrests, lawyers pimping for business and post mortem after post mortem. The only counselling we had then was a slap on the back and words of encouragement like: "No worries, mate. Have another tinny." For the next six weeks we travelled round the outback of Oz like one big family, laughing and joking all the way and without a care in the world. It was a surreal six weeks where rarely a cross word was uttered and both romances and friendships blossomed.

We began to enjoy our crappy little coach, arriving at tourist spots and squeezing into the parking bays between two shiny, deluxe tour buses. Other stunned tourists and bus drivers would stare at our motley group. We must have emitted some positivity or maybe possessed a captivating aura because we had recently escaped death. Many strangers would gravitate towards us. They would come up to us and start talking and joking with us. There would be an air of light-heartedness and bonhomie.

On our bus, we developed a social hierarchy and a pecking order. Jock and Lottie were the much revered group elders and brought a sense of order to the younger crew. They acted as the kindly grand-parents on the bus. Margie and Doris were two mature nurses taking a trip away from their families. They became the mothers of the coach and the medics diagnosing most minor illnesses and dispensing a seemingly endless array of pills and ointments, but specialising in hangover cures. The rest were an odd assortment, each on the tour for a different reason.

Then there was Jim, a telecoms expert from London who on holiday. Jim was different from the rest and tended to keep himself to himself. His shyness was wrongly identified as not wanting to mix with the rest and he ashamedly became the whipping horse for any practical joke, such as placing orange peel in the space between his spectacles and his eyes whilst he was asleep.

The two Scottish girls had joined the tour as they had nothing better to do. One was dumpy and jolly, the other was dumpy but not so jolly. They both spoke with a soft Lowland accent. When we were travelling through the outback and the huge red form of Ayers Rock came into view, they jumped up and shrieked with excitement:

"Heavens, that's a muckle chuckie!" (Scottish for big pebble).

The tour developed into a storyline from a soap opera. Liaisons came and went. Christopher fancied Margie and Margie may have fancied Christopher. Paul still liked Libby and Kev still liked Joanna and vice versa. Jock and Lotty continued to prepare for their Diamond Anniversary. The coach drivers' dalliances were numerous and supposedly secret. But there were no secrets within the group. We knew everything, except, that is, of what the two Scottish girls were up to. No one had the faintest idea.

When the tour came to an end, there was a sense of loss as we parted. We seemed to have been through a lot. Some of us kept in touch for many years after.

After the tour, bus trips for me in Australia seemed to get worse. The most uncomfortable was a 60-hour journey from Sydney to Perth. There was no air conditioning and the tedium of crossing the Nullabor Plain came close to inducing madness. The one excitement was watching the changeover of drivers which they did while the bus was doing 50mph without slowing down. It was masterful to watch, like some well choreographed ballet as one driver took his foot off the accelerator and the other reached round behind and replaced it with his own foot. It was the Aussie bus drivers' equivalent to playing *Twister*.

The roads ran straight for hundreds of miles at a time so there was little chance of hitting very much, except for the odd crossing kangaroo. It was a dirty journey, too, as the red dust seemed to find a way into everything. At wash stops the water was so hard that no soap would lather and unless there was a special kind of soap, there was little point in washing. Seeing the outskirts of Perth was a momentous event. I've never enjoyed a shower in the hotel more, and I stood under the water jets for half an hour. I came out looking like a wrinkled prune, but I was perfumed and felt human again.

It was the wrong assumption to think that buses in New Zealand would be more genteel. The first morning I had to take the bus to my new place of work at Aulsebrooks Biscuits (now no more, having been taken over by Arnotts) in the suburb of Otahuhu, on the southside of Auckland. Otahuhu in 1980 was a volatile melting pot of islanders from the South Pacific. There were Samoans, Fijians, Tongans, Polynesians and practically every other islander living and working there. The buses were old, generally driven by fearsome women, often Maoris who stood for no nonsense and there was the smell of burnt out clutch throughout the bus. On boarding the lady driver gave me a murderous looking stare. She watched me in the interior mirror, slammed the door shut and floored the accelerator pedal, sending me crashing down the aisle to the back seat.

I learnt fast.

The next morning when the same lady driver stopped at the bus stop, I leapt on and ran down the aisle to the nearest seat. It spoilt her fun. She never stopped trying and would try to send me flying by driving off before the doors were closed. It turned into a game of cat and mouse, but I felt I had the upper hand and gradually her murderous look, changed to a mischievous grin. One morning after her widest smile yet, I decided that the next trip I would try to strike up a conversation with her. But it was a different driver. I never saw her again and a part of me regretted not speaking up earlier.

In Asia, buses were the lifeblood of most countries and the only way to travel. I was to find being a tall Da Bize (Big Nose) or Gweilo (Foreign Devil) to be a disadvantage. Chinese buses were cramped and overflowing. If you stood up for even the briefest moments, someone would steal your seat. This had the effect of sending my travelling companion apoplectic. Being of a fearless nature, she physically evicted the offender. But when she turned round again and tried to sit, another person had grabbed her seat. After the twenty-second time even she had to admit defeat.

The Chinese drivers were fastidious with timekeeping. A private bus we once took to the airport became an exasperating experience. The hotel had given the driver precise instructions that we should arrive at the airport at 12 noon. In the Chinese mind 12 noon meant 12 noon. Not five to. Not five past. The driver sped like a scalded cat for two hours before realising that he was going to be far too early. The remaining hour was driven at 20mph and there was no point in complaining. It changed nothing. We arrived on the dot of 12pm.

In Burma they were even more crowded. When the bus was full, the duck seller would force his way on with bamboo crates full of live birds. As in all parts of Asia, bus drivers headed at full speed up the middle of the road, stopping for no one and hooting their horn as they went. The tropical monsoon storms were so bad in Malaysia that the bus aquaplaned along the rain sodden roads all through the journey. The drivers had the habit of driving faster, perhaps in the belief that their bus would get a good wash.

The Philippines lived up to every preconception and expectation. The colour of the Jeepneys, the overcrowded buses with twenty people sitting on the roof, the narrow and twisty roads all contributed to making travelling interesting and difficult when the rains came.

"What's that down there?" I asked the lady sitting next door to me, pointing at a silver glint at the bottom of the ravine, in the river several hundred feet below. "Oh that was a bus that did not make the corner," she said taking a puff on her pipe. "Nobody made it." I wasn't concerned as I had been sitting next to this lady for eleven hours and was getting used to her bluntness. She was a doctor returning home and earlier we had been talking about the poisonous snakes I was likely to see around the village I was going to.

"I suppose the hospital is well stocked with anti-venom."

"Oh not at all," she replied.

"Then what happens?"

"Well," she smiled and looked me directly in the eye before adding, "that's it." I returned my gaze to the lit up model of the Virgin Mary on the dashboard of the bus. Above it and surrounded by aromatic white flowers which are usually found near any Asian graveyard was a poster saying 'God Bless Our Trip'. I silently agreed.

"And before you ask about the large number of rocks and the fact that the road has disappeared," she pre-empted my inquisitiveness. "that was just the recent eruption of Mount Pinatubo." She laughed and pointed towards the religious poster at the front of the bus.

The Philippines is a predominantly Catholic country with over 80% claiming to be a member of the Roman Catholic Church. Nearly everywhere I went there were religious artefacts or words or prayers. This was prevalent in any form public transport, on the Jeepneys and the buses in particular. The model statues of the saints which adorned the dashboards seemed to have little effect on the average standard of driving.

Taking the night bus to the northern province of Ilocos Norte in

North Luzon was a bitter sweet experience. It was hot and cramped. The many stops made it difficult to sleep. There was a choice of several bus companies, and everyone in the Philippines had their own pet bus company. The person I travelled with liked a company called Maria de Leon because the drivers were local Ilocanos who lived in the same village, dropping passengers off close to their houses. As a result, Maria de Leon had developed a strong local following by offering a door-to-door service.

I always preferred taking the buses which were not fitted with air conditioning. With all the windows opened to attract the cooler night air, it felt like I was entering an alternative world which I would have missed in an air conditioned express bus. No town ever slept and there was a hive of selling activity around the bus stations, from individually wrapped sweets to single cigarettes to any kind of food. At 3am the bus halted outside the fresh kill butcher. The beasts were killed behind a shed and the meat was quickly butchered and sold to passing bus travellers.

I went on this marathon bus journey with a seventy year old Filipina called Emilia, who lived a quiet life in a small village called Lanao, keeping pigs, cultivating rice and threatening to retire. Village life was not so tranquil. As soon as the sun's first rays lit the dawn sky, the cocks crew, every house turned its radio on to full volume and boys started castigating their goats and caribou as they led them to new pasture. The bell would sound at the local Catholic church as a call to mass. The bell was an old Japanese bomb casing from the Second World War which Father Fernandez enthusiastically hit to rally the villagers.

Another form of transport the Filipinos relied on was the ubiquitous Jeepney. It was designed from the blueprint of the World War II American Jeep, out of which came this strange looking aluminium mini bus. The design has changed little in 60 years. They were individually named and decorated by their owners.

Emilia, when she retired, had bought a Jeepney which she called London Express to run as a commercial service to the nearest town, Laoag City. When London Express was not on service duty, it would go to the rice fields and carry sacks of newly harvested rice. Occasionally it was used as a vehicle to transport the many members of her family and friends in her village.

Some of her relations thought it might be a good idea to take me on an adventure in some of the wildest, most mountainous and inhospitable terrain in the province. The problem was that they had not been there very often as it carried a reputation of being bandit country. But it seemed a good excuse for them to fill London Express with what seemed to be most of the male members of the village who wanted a day out. The vehicle was well stocked with beer, gin and a little food and we were heavily laden before we climbed the first mountain track.

It was a fantastic day, through some of the most beautiful country I had ever seen. There were numerous stops at churches, gardens and even a tilapia fish farm they had wanted to visit for years, which were only really excuses to crack open the gin bottle and wash it down with a beer. London Express with its regular driver Bidi (pronounced Beady) performed well at first. But the higher we climbed into the mountains, the worse the roads became until they were dirt tracks. Even these petered out where they had been washed away by the monsoon rain.

We came to a fast flowing river. Bidi was more used to driving on concrete roads. The local Jeepney drivers took the river at speed and kept their foot down, spray engulfing the passengers who were sitting on the roof. Bidi however was nervous and drove slowly. We sank. Great glee came from the passing Jeepneys, their passengers cheering and horns blaring. They never stopped. They couldn't or they would have got bogged too. We dug. Bidi tentatively went forward. We sank again. We dug. We sank deeper. It took two hours to dig ourselves out, requiring an elongated gin stop before returning to the village.

Poor old London Express returned to the village in a sorry state. Mud caked, exhaust-less and with a broken clutch she limped back to her home. The people on board looked even worse. That was the first and last adventure London Express went on. She never recovered after that and was confined to taxi work and carrying bags of rice from the paddy fields to the house for drying. Only rarely did she go further, to the market in Manila, crammed with bags of red rice. In a short time the taxi work dried up, owing to the market being flooded with Jeepneys all travelling to the same place at the same time. The only option for Emilia was to sell London Express.

My first physical involvement with driving buses came when I had the wild idea of taking an accessible bus out to Poland to be used by a group of disabled people in Sopot, close to Gdansk. It was 1989. The Berlin Wall had just come down. Disabled people in the Communist era in Poland had suffered over the past decades. They were viewed as a national disgrace and often kept indoors. In the many times I had visited the country with my mother, who had started a charity called Help Poland in 1981 taking medical supplies and aid to hospitals and churches all over Poland , rarely did I see a wheelchair on the streets. It was as if people were ashamed or frightened of any disability.

The Big Red Bus project, as it was called, never came to fruition. The disabled access Leyland National ex Mobility bus, generously donated by London Transport, failed its emissions test and a certificate of roadworthiness was refused by the Ministry in Warsaw. It was a pity – everything was ready. I had even been given a driving assessment by Kentish Bus. It was my first time behind the wheel of a bus and though I didn't need a licence at that time as I would not be carrying any fare paying passengers, it was thought advisable that I should gain some experience and I quite fancied having a go at driving a bus.

"Cup of tea," bellowed the instructor.

"Yes please," I said as we were proceeding around a trading estate in Gravesend. He glared but remained silent.

"Cup of tea," he repeated at the next corner. He was to say this phrase over fifty times during the one hour assessment. At the end I summoned up the courage to ask him why he kept saying "cup of tea" when there was no sign of any cafe or canteen along the route.

"Fear not," he grinned "I say it to everyone. Every time you hit a kerb you owe me a cup of tea. It gets expensive and you currently owe me fifty-two cups." He did go on to say that with practice I would improve. But I was doing this only with the single aim of being able to drive the Big Red Bus to Sopot. I would never need my bus licence for anything else.

I should have realised that emissions were going to be a problem when we took the Big Red Bus on a fundraising exercise to the Richmond Dog Show, held annually in the Silver Ring at Ascot Racecourse. The organisers allowed the bus to be parked amongst the trade stands and to collect money. It was a hot and balmy September weekend and we were looking forward to raising substantial funds.

Disaster occurred. At teatime, for some unknown reason, I thought it would be a good idea to turn the engine over and run it for a few minutes. I didn't realise that older buses can sometimes misbehave and if I had looked in the wing mirrors whilst revving the sluggish engine, I would surely have noticed several people running out of the thick black diesel smoke which filled the adjacent stall. They were bent double, coughing and looking queasy. If I had not revved the engine so energetically then perhaps I would also have heard the angry voices and the increased swearing as yet more thick black smoke billowed out of the Big Red Bus's exhaust.

It was the irate stall holder who recovered fastest from the attempt to asphyxiate him and his customers and he proceeded to take out his poor humour on the automatic doors, breaking them down and looking as if he wished to asphyxiate me. The fundraising came to an abrupt halt. We had raised £3.46p and a couple of Irish pennies.

Eight years later and I had mysteriously fallen into the bus industry. The subject of emissions reared its head again in the first days of working for a company based in Cumbria and Tyneside. One of the drivers from their depot on the outskirts of Newcastle explained in detail how I should follow his example and asphyxiate other car drivers and pedestrians on the road, professionally and proficiently.

"Do you know how to POLLUTE someone?" Pete had casually asked one day while we sat waiting for the rugby club to return to the bus after their post match marathon drinking session.

He continued without waiting for me to answer, "I was on a single track in this old Volvo bus in the Lake District when over the hill came this open-topped sports car. The driver was fuming and refused to reverse. It was a stalemate as I wasn't going to reverse so I stood there. Having threatened me and continually shouted at me I still refused to budge. After 20 minutes, he angrily threw his car into reverse until, quite some distance away he backed into a passing place. As I went past – he let fly again. Every word was preceded with an f or a b. So when he stopped I quietly said to him – Have you ever been polluted?"

"No, the sports car driver said to me, a little more nervously this time. No I haven't actually – what do you mean polluted????"

Peter drove on slowly past the car. On the old Volvos there is a button marked – **COLD START** which is meant to be used on cold mornings to help start the bus. By pressing this button a valve is released a load of diesel is dumped into the engine and the fuel ignites faster. If you press this button when the engine is warm and running, a remarkable event takes place.

He looked in his wing mirror and when he saw that his exhaust was aligned with the sports car driver, he revved his engine and simultaneously pushed the **COLD START** button. A mushroom cloud of thick, sulphurous and foul smelling fumes belched out of the exhaust and enveloped the sports car.

Sensibly Pete decided not to hang around. As the clouds began to clear, he thought he saw a still furious but visibly shaken figure, hair ruffled and covered in a thin film of black smog.

"The moral of the story is never be rude to a bus driver," he advised.

* * * * * *

Long before even thinking about becoming a bus driver, I decided to take my HGV (Heavy Goods Vehicle) licence. I had no desire to be a truck driver for a career but thought it would be useful for driving medical supplies to Poland for my mother's charity. She was always looking out for drivers. It was becoming harder to find volunteer drivers who offered their services for free. So it made sense for me to hold a licence.

On past trips to Poland no licence seemed to be necessary as the Polish Militja took little notice of what type of driving licence you held, as long as it was an International Driving Licence. When they stopped you, they were usually looking for a few US$ as a bribe. The main difficulty was getting from our depot at Hatfield, around the newly built M25 to Purfleet Deepwater Dock, where the Polish Ocean Lines cargo ship, the SS Inowrocklaw left for Gdynia.

Not having a British HGV licence meant that we had to risk it, and drive illegally to the port. We would leave our base in the early hours and drove like fury with half an ear cocked at Sheila Tracy's Truckers Hour on Radio 2. Professional truck drivers who drove to Poland assured us this was the perfect time to travel as it was the time the police went for their tea breaks and the roads were left unpatrolled. It sounded dubious advice, but we were fortunate and never got caught.

The trips started in 1981, via the DFDS ferry from Harwich to Hamburg, through the DDR (East Germany) to Berlin and across the Polish border at Frankfurt-am-Oder. The first stop in Berlin was near calamitous. Our naivety in driving the trucks through Checkpoint Charlie caused a diplomatic incident and resulted in being shouted at by German police, French, British and American soldiers simultaneously in their mother tongues. It was chaotic. The checkpoint was a chicane in the shape of an exaggerated zig-zag with concrete barriers on all sides and corners. It was designed for light traffic. The 40ft articulated truck became wedged. The East German watchtower on the other side of the Wall became a hive of activity. It usually contained no more than a handful of guards, but now had dozens of East German border guards pushing and shoving each other in an eager attempt to see what the commotion was.

It took one hour to extricate the truck and reverse back on to the main road.

It took another fifteen years for me to do something about getting an HGV licence. I chose the Scottish Borders not for its scenic beauty, but for the fact that the driving test examiners, at that time, permitted learners to practise on the same roads that the test route followed. Familiarity was a confidence booster. The only obstacle was whether you had the notorious examiner, Gale Force George to oversee your driving test. It was a one in three chance.

The day of the test arrived and to my horror I spotted Gale Force George getting out of his car at the car park. My legs wilted beneath me, turning to jelly and my knees started knocking. He looked like a French detective standing there in his waterproof macintosh in the drizzle and dreech, waiting to question every aspect of me, leaving no stone unturned. I would soon find out how much of a reality George's feared reputation and whether his nickname was correct in describing the habit he was alleged to have of moving fast around the cab so that he did not miss anything the driver was doing. Some learners had found this distracting.

The test seemed to be going well. I followed his instructions to the T. I had negotiated all the hazards. I had not been put off by the boy racers in their lowered suspension cars blasting out gangsta rap through their deep thumping stereos systems. Nor was I put off by the pungent smell of deep fried haggis and Mars bars which wafted out of the chippy situated next to the traffic lights which seemed to take an age to turn green. Everything George asked me to do, I did, and I did well. He sat perfectly still and I was beginning to think his reputation was a tall story.

Then things went rapidly downhill on a steep part of the town. The corner had a reputation as being the scene of many test failures. The wall was too high to see if there were any cars coming out of the side road. They tended to come late and just as you had committed to the right turn. It meant the truck was stranded in the middle of the road with no room for you or the other vehicle to get round the corner or past each other. The examiner would judge this to be your fault and a fail-able offence. Naturally a car did come late and though I was only inching down the hill I still had to break quite sharply. The calm and confident atmosphere changed and I noticed George sat more upright and seemed to be scrutinising me more.

Then disaster struck on another bad corner in Selkirk. I braked too sharply when a car pulled out in front of me without looking. George produced a theatrical performance of Shakespearian pro-portions as he slammed into the windscreen. He was flung or flung himself forwards with far greater force than was necessary and ended up with his nose and hands, still clasping the pen and clipboard, pressed against the glass. His glasses were at 45 degrees and he took slow, deliberate steps to return to his usual immaculate image. He dusted himself down, straightened his tie, combed his hair and returned the clipboard to its rightful place on his lap. "Holy Moses! That's it, I've failed", I muttered rather too loudly. I gloomily drove back to the car park. "You've passed," said Gale Force George in an unemotional way. I fainted.

* * * * * *

Several weeks later I had a job and was let loose on the highways. On my first journey a dented white Ford Transit van stopped in front of my parked truck at Forton Services on the M6 in Lancashire. The driver was a thick set bloke with a bald head, except for a small line of hair which ran towards his collar. He wore a knee-length brown leather coat and motorbike boots. He oozed menace as he came up to my window. I nervously wound it down, expecting trouble. He looked left and right, surveying the busy HGV park before beginning to talk.

"Psst! Hey mate," his voice was close to a falsetto voice with added Lancashire accent and his hard man image was dashed instantaneously. "Do you want to buy any tools?" It was hard to stop my imagination running riot to discover what might have made him talk in the way he did.

Whatever the reason was, it had the effect of relieving the boredom I had so far experienced driving a truck that day. Becoming a truck driver had been a baptism of fire. I was not used to the early starts. It had commenced at 3am in a warehouse of a well-known department store. It had not improved by trundling up various motorways for four hours at 55mph. I had unhitched the trailer and was waiting for another lorry to arrive from somewhere 'down south' before having to drive another four hours up the same motorways.

Service station car parks were similar to bazaars. Travelling salesmen abounded and strange looking vans, often with Irish number plates cruised round the parked trucks selling their wares. This week it was tools, last week it was kitchen knives and Korean condoms, the week before it was pink satin lingerie and brand new Barbour waxed jackets, hot from the factory. Things were supposedly so hot that it was not unusual to see policemen checking the car parks, sending the salesmen diving back into their vans mid sale and screeching away.

The romantic illusion of being a volunteer truck driver in Poland was long gone. Having nothing better to do, I started HGV driving professionally in England. The experience of being sat in the cab of a truck, lorry or, wagon for long periods of time at a governed speed, mainly at night was a shock to the system. The monotony was relieved by having the radio on permanently and the occasional unusual events which occurred.

I turned first to a driving agency. I was the lowest of the low. Transport Managers would often refer to me as 'just another bloody agency driver.' At the beginning driving 40-foot articulated wagons was terrifying. I made many horrendous mistakes. My first was when delivering to a tea company's premises in the North East. The sun was hovering low over the factory roof, and though astoundingly beautiful, it made it impossible to see anything while reversing, particularly into the dark hole of the loading bay. There was a CRUNCH followed by the unbearable sound of metal scraping against metal. Two metal reflective strips protecting the concrete walls of the loading bay fell to the ground in a twisted and mangled state. On the plus side they had done what they were supposed to do. I obviously hadn't.

Seemingly out of nowhere, a mini-army of people appeared from all corners of the factory. Some came equipped with clipboards, some with cameras, some with dictaphones but all in white lab coats and hard hats and all with mobile phones glued to their ears and speaking in urgent tones to the person on the other end. I felt like a criminal and I felt like a naughty schoolboy who had been summoned to appear in front of the headmaster to explain my misdemeanours.

For goodness sake, I thought, they were only two insignificant pieces of aluminium and the wagon only had a small dent in it. This incident turned out to be my induction to the then new Health and Safety at Work laws which were starting to be implemented more stringently at that time. It felt a little over zealous, but in hindsight it was a snapshot of what was going to happen over the following years and become a standard throughout Britain.

Then there was the unfortunate early morning episode whilst hitching up a truck to a trailer by the side of a misty River Tyne which so nearly ended in embarrassing disaster. The most basic of rules drummed into recently qualified truck drivers was that they should, without fail, always engage the handbrake when stopping and particularly when hitching up the air lines between the cab and the trailer.

I neglected to do this. While I was standing on the rear of the cab and congratulating myself on such a clean and efficient job as I connected the last hose – the truck and trailer started to move forwards. It started gently, slowly rolling then hurriedly picked up speed on the downward slope. Faster and faster it went. Momentarily I froze as the full implications of impending disaster sank in and I looked over the cab roof to see the front of other parked trailers coming sharply into view.

I jumped off awkwardly and started running alongside the cab. My heart was thumping and I felt an ever increasing sense of alarm and panic with the realisation that the vehicle was outrunning me. There was one last option. I tried an ungainly Tarzanesque leap and sprang up on to the driver's side door. With incredible luck I made it, thanks to the window being wound down which allowed my long arms to reach into the cab and pull on the handbrake. With a scrunching of gravel and voluble hissing the truck came to an abrupt halt, no more than ten feet away from the facing trailer.

Sweating profusely, shaking and breathing out a huge blow of relief I sat thinking of what would have happened if there had been an accident. What would I have told the Transport Manager and how would I have explained that there had been a crash – basically through my own negligence? Failed brakes? Mist clogged up the air lines? Mud on the road? No I came to the conclusion that the Transport Manager had heard it all before and that the only viable solution was to come clean. The phrase 'just another bloody agency driver' for some reason kept reverberating around inside my head.

I went on to drive for a distribution company which had a contract to supply a leading supermarket with their goods. This was like going back to school. The enormous depot, based less than a mile from the M25, had constant traffic. Trucks coming in and going out; twenty four hours a day; everyday. Special loaders with flashing orange lights and warning sirens moved empty and full trailers between the warehouse and their respective parking lots. This was a military operation. It had to be – otherwise the supermarkets could not operate. I had the feeling that I was being institutionalised.

I signed in at the traffic office and waited for my name to be called out. A truck was allocated and papers were given out detailing which trailer to connect to, where it was parked, directions of how to reach the supermarket you were delivering to and the time slot you were expected to arrive at. If this slot was missed the supermarket would have sent the truck back to the depot as it would have upset the schedule for other delivery trucks. Sometimes a new delivery slot would be arranged and sometimes the cargo would have to be destroyed because it did not meet trading standards requirements anymore and the supermarket would have refused to accept it. All in all it was a costly business. A mere five minutes could cost thousands.

There were long periods of waiting around. You never knew when you would be called. I waited in a room which was the size of a tennis court. It was abuzz with other drivers playing pool, darts, eating, reading or chatting as they waited for the loudspeaker to announce their name. It was a soulless room with a canteen, some chairs and many food and drinks vending machines stationed around the outsides. The irritating sound of one-armed bandits was always present above the sound of voices.

There was a surprising undercurrent of nervousness about the place. The other drivers would mask it by exhibiting bravado and talking loudly or telling blue jokes. I found I could never fully relax. The fear of not hearing your name as it was read out put me constantly on edge. You never really got to know the other drivers. There were so many of them and agency drivers came and went on a daily basis, and of course, were still viewed as being a carbuncle in a well oiled machine.

Night work, though well paid was even more soulless at the depot. Nobody talked to each other much. Arriving at the supermarket was considerably better as there was a scaled down staff who were more relaxed and not under so much pressure as their 9-5 colleagues. They had time to talk to the drivers. Also the traffic was far less and the roads were clear.

Daytime was sometimes impossible and some of the supermarkets had been designed with maximum floor area for customers and minimal turning space for wagons. It was a constant battle to avoid metal delivery trolleys, rubbish bins, recycling, plastic, cars, other trucks and gates. The staff would park their cars blocking the entrance and would complain vociferously when their wing mirrors were hit by passing delivery wagons.

One day I was sent to a supermarket in a busy Essex town. I managed to avoid the parked staff cars but I did not manage to avoid the gates. In fact I reversed into them. My extenuating circumstances were that it was not totally my fault, as I was aided in my crime by a junior store-man who guided me back.

"You will tell me when I am near the gates, won't you?" I asked him.

"Yes, of course I will," he replied indignantly. "Back ... back ... back ..."

CRASH!

The supermarket employee shuffled back to the cab, smiled and cheerily said: "That will be the gates."

I felt my bonus fading away. Instead I drove away fuming and determined never again to trust a member of the public, supermarket worker, or any other worker to guide you back. That was until the next time.

After supermarkets, I was a general courier delivery driver. A white van man, but in a truck. I had an embarrassing problem with the first truck I was assigned. It kept slowing down and trying to stop. I lost touch with the amount of times I took it back to the maintenance depot and the mechanics grew progressively tired and dismayed as they never found any fault.

I solved the mystery, by chance one night on the M62, close to the summit of the Pennines. The truck was in perfect working order. It was the heel of my Size 15s which was causing the problem. Being a newly qualified truck driver no one had given me a guided tour around the cab. Everyone assumed that all drivers should know there was a small button directly under the driver's seat which when depressed started the exhaust brake. "Just another bloody agency driver," rang around my head again.

I regularly delivered a magazine, the *Auto Trader*, picking it up from the printers in the North West and delivering it to the wholesalers at Stockton, Sunderland, Durham and Newcastle. Likewise the *Daily* and *Sunday Mirror* and the *Newcastle Chronicle*. Behind the scenes was a hive of activity as you waited for the publications to roll off the presses. Heavy bundles of newspapers would appear wrapped in brown paper and tied together with white binder twine. They still smelled of printing press oil. The atmosphere amongst drivers and printers was electric and vans were buzzing about all over the place. The experienced hands drove as if they had ants in their pants, desperate to deliver and get back to bed.

I worked as a courier driver for a major courier, overnight delivery and logistics companies, alternating between smaller trucks and articulated lorries. It was a pressurised job as most parcels had to be somewhere by a certain time or penalties ensued. There was the constant fear of outrunning traffic wardens and police as the only parking spaces were on double yellow lines. Many times I was ticketed. I drew the short straw and seemed to always be given the job of delivering to a sewage farm. After each visit it took hours to remove the awful smell from my clothes.

After one of these visits I had a delivery at a merchant bank in the centre of Newcastle. The person who took the parcel knew me. As a matter of fact we had had dinner with a mutual friend the previous week. He took one look at me and went pale as I handed him the parcel and asked him to sign the docket. Initially I thought his reaction was his surprise at seeing me doing this job and that I was a courier driver, but on reflection it was more likely that he was overcome by the stink.

I also delivered building supplies for a plumbers' merchant. I visited every new building site and housing development in the region. Some house builders had it down to a fine art and could put up a house in three days but the quality of the materials being used was poor. Once I was delivering a basin to the upstairs bathroom of a new build. Halfway up the stairs I overbalanced and the basin and I went straight through the thin wall and ended up in the living room. I never had the guts to own up, but rather like a *Tom and Jerry* cartoon, I suspect my bulky shape left its imprint on the wall for all to see. Amazingly no one ever questioned me about the damage.

I went on to gain my ADR Licence which enabled me to carry all kinds of toxic and nasty chemicals. I was qualified to carry any chemical or fuel including explosives and radioactive materials though I rarely used it. Embedded in my mind for evermore during training was the Instructor's description of what to do in an emergency when there is a chemical spill. 'Rule No 1 – Look after yourself, so lick your finger, stick it up in the air, gauge the wind direction and RUN LIKE F--K IN THE OPPOSITE DIRECTION'.

Having been through the training, I have become a truck spotter. Not actually trucks, but the plaque with the picture telling people whether it was corrosive, explosive or hazardous. It also contained a number which details the actual substance or chemical. If it was the number which denoted a nasty chemical such as phenol, I would tend to give the truck a wide berth and put my foot down.

The last trucking job I could stick was delivering bog rolls to wholesalers and supermarkets nationwide. The boredom was so intense and the hours so long that I often had to park in a lay-by and sleep in the truck. The top layer of bog rolls would sometimes arrive at their destination with a dent in them, as I had used them as my mattress rather than having to suffer the cold and uncomfortable cab.

The very worst job was when my wife Pauline was in the last stages of pregnancy and it was too risky for me to drive at night in case she went into labour. So instead I went and worked night shifts in the bog roll factory warehouse, 20 minutes' drive away. The shift of nine hours consisted of splitting up the rolls on one pallet and making a bigger pile on another, larger pallet. It was backbreaking and deadly dull. Bog rolls in quantity were deceptively heavy. The radio was turned up to full volume so that the fork lift drivers could hear the inane chat of the late night phone in called Alan Robson's Night Owls programme, above the noise of their engines.

I finally saw the red light and called time on my truck driving career. While delivering a gasket to my old friend the sewage farm, I tripped and caught my hand on the side of the trailer before falling into a pile of foul smelling brown earth. Not only did I smell worse than usual, but my hand was bleeding badly and I had to borrow an assortment of oily rags to form a tourniquet. I drove back one and a half handed to the depot, where the Transport Manager following the usual greeting of "just another bloody agency driver" showed an abundance of sympathy and kindness. It did not take long to realise that he was petrified I would turn round and sue.

There and then I suddenly had the impulsive desire to acquire a bus driving licence. Why? I have no idea. I don't think I will ever know. Folie de grandeur? Showing off? Perhaps it was a natural progression for a truck driver. Perhaps it was sheer desperation. For certain it was by accident. The reality was that I found myself back in the Scottish Borders. And guess who should get out of the car in the car park to examine my driving but Gale Force George? The morning had started badly when the bus my driving instructor had borrowed from a local bus company had failed to appear. It was the same bus I had learnt on for the previous four days and the thought of having to take the test in a replacement and unfamiliar bus filled me with dread. My instructor looked at his boots, turned a little pink and explained that the bus had been on a school run and had run out of diesel. A mechanic worked a miracle and the bus arrived in the car park at exactly the same moment that George was walking across the tarmac.

The relief was indescribable. I was on such a high that I drove spectacularly well. 'You've passed, again' he said again in his monotone. Now I was able to seek employment in the bus industry. It was an exciting and a frightening thought. It was a far more frightening thought for my future passengers. They were going to be truly terrified.

CHAPTER 2

A NEW BUS DRIVER –
TEETHING PROBLEMS

The first thing I was told by the veteran bus drivers was that newly qualified drivers in their first year make all the stupid and mundane mistakes there are to make. I was not going to be an exception to the rule but there was no point worrying about it. I had to find a job first.

It was a revelation when looking through the jobs section of the *Newcastle Journal*, to find that a bus company based in the North East needed drivers and that experience was not essential. Most adverts I had scoured had required applicants to have had at least two years' driving experience. This company was based in an industrial area close to the River Tyne. The depot in the remains of an old iron foundry was just off a busy roundabout which, as I was to discover towards the end of my employment, had the reputation of being car thieves' favourite escape route via the nearby bridge over the river. There were spates of crime of which car theft was the premier activity.

To the naïve novice such as myself, the bus company seemed to have a secure and trustworthy ring to it. It was an old and reputable company, with a strong name and with a seemingly good history to it. It all sounded very promising. The reality was somewhat different and if it had not been my first interview for a bus driver's job, I am sure I would have run a mile. They were so welcoming and almost laid out the red carpet which, I maybe should have spotted, was masking their financial situation and that they were so desperate for drivers that they would accept more or less anyone.

Perhaps they looked at me and thought "there's no fool like an old fool".

The town in which the company was based had the air of being a once prosperous industrial hub. Now there was not any evidence of even faded grandeur. It was just a poor commuter town with a fish and chip shop being its most famous attraction. The river, by the time it had reached this far downstream, had lost its earlier promise of beauty and had become a repository for any unwanted household waste. The depot itself was messy and old buses in red, white and blue livery were parked around the yard. The place had a strange atmosphere. The buildings were dilapidated, the drivers who I met seemed genuine, though they housed a devil-may-care attitude. The transport manager seemed to be permanently on the phone, chasing up drivers to come into work and the MD cursed an awful lot between the smiles.

But I was new. As far as I knew, anywhere in the bus world would be a good place to cut my teeth.

Perhaps I should also have spotted the clue on the notice boards in the drivers' rest room. In the middle was a large sign advertising the services the coach company offered. It had been defaced by one of the drivers who had written over the poster in thick black marker pen saying:

Welcome!
Expect
Unreasonable
Wages

Don't expect
Any
Time off

I was interviewed by a driver. He talked more about the times he sent European air traffic controllers into a rage in an attempts at strike busting than he did about the bus company. Once when he was in the air the complete network came to a halt as the controllers announced that they were on strike and from immediate effect all airports were closed.

"He told me I would have to turn back and go home," said the driver. "Right, I thought, I will find a way. I wasn't going to turn round. No way."

His opportunity arrived in the shape of a military jet which, flying below him and about to land at the nearest airport. He dived and followed directly behind in its jet stream. The fighter jet landed and seconds later his plane landed, before the controllers realised what was going on.

"It was lovely," he said. "The Gallic swear words which came flooding into my headphones were choice. But there was nothing they could do about it. We won."

My interview lasted a matter of minutes.

"Can you drive?"

"Yes"

"Driven much? "

"A little. "

"Great," and I was told that I had a job subject to the result of a trial drive. It consisted of driving with the senior fitter standing beside me, in what turned out to be once round the block, leaving the depot car park – up the dual carriageway ramp, to the next roundabout, around it and back into the depot. It took all of 5 minutes.

"Cushti," said the accompanying mechanic, on our return to the office. "He'll do nicely!" From the first day I drove for them, it became apparent that the company was in financial trouble. This was made worse by what seemed to be a permanent shortage of drivers. I began to suspect that the peculiar rag-bag assortment of drivers who were with the company had been lured off the nearby dual carriageway into the depot and treated to as minimal a job interview as I had been. They were a good bunch though, with the usual Geordie bus depot humour combined with hot-headedness and grumpiness in equal measures, particularly when they were suffering from a hangover, which was not an unusual occurrence.

Amongst the more experienced drivers there was an initial shock and suspicion, when they saw me, that, either the boss had lost his marbles and given a complete and utter oddball a job, or he had sent in a spy. The verdict was open. They couldn't decide. Here was a near two-metre giant with a 'posh accent' who obviously was wet behind the ears and knew nothing about driving buses. From day one they were kind to me and pushed me in the right direction by answering my idiotic questions.

"Why can I not get this bus to start?" I would ask in a blind panic, having tried for ten minutes without success and with the fear of being late.

"You haven't turned the isolator switch on. Try it. It's situated down and to the right of the seat on most buses."

It started immediately.

Slowly I was accepted into their ranks. I knew that the ice had been broken and that I had made friends when I was asked a few months later to join the drivers on a 'big night out' at the bars and pubs in a suburb of Gateshead. Eight pubs later and having lost count of how many pints had been sunk, it was hard to remember very much, though two things did stick in my mind. One was the vaguest recollection of two people (not in our group) standing in the middle of the road smashing beer bottles over each other's heads.

The other was one of the bus driver's friends whose job was a train driver, giving me friendly advice of what to do the moment you see a person standing in the middle of the tracks, if I ever decided to change jobs and drive a train.

"Oh it must be simply terrifying. What do you do? Brake, I suppose," I said in what must have been a condescending tone, expecting the driver to concur and talk about the trauma of it all and the counselling that must follow.

"Nothing like that," he replied. "We put the foot down so we can collect the money!'"

"Money?" I said feebly. "What money?"

"The compensation money, of course. We get good money for the trauma and psychological damage."

The driver's rest room in the depot was the meeting place at the beginning and end of shifts, unless you had to drive to a remote bus stop and relieve another driver at the end of his shift. It was a cold room with a kettle, some lockers, a notice board with various rude messages attached to the memos sent from management and the duty roster. The magnolia paint was flaking off the walls and there was an aroma of rising damp, diesel, engine oil and bus drivers.

The usual friendly greeting was a grunt and a subdued "Good Morning", "Good Afternoon" or "Good Evening". It was sometimes hushed by the sound of a driver entering and letting off a loud fart. The average diet of a plate of chips and curry sauce from the fish and chip shop across the road from the depot, which was a ritual amongst drivers at the end of a long shift the night before was usually to blame.

Loud, uncontrolled farting was prevalent at all bus depots I worked at and seemed to either be a comic device or a way of coping with the stresses of the job. I couldn't decide which. Likewise the jokes were the same, many had an Irish theme. There was always someone holding court, I dreaded hearing "come here, you've gotta hear this one." Naturally the favourite joke was often produced which involved Irishmen breaking into a bus depot and taking the wrong bus following a long night on the tiles. Hoots of laughter always rang around the driver's room when the punchline: "Can't find the No. 8? We'll just have to take the No.11. It goes as far as the round-about and we'll walk from there," was delivered.

Though they might not have been side splittingly funny, the jokes and light-hearted banter I soon learned acted like a release valve to counterbalance the accumulated pressure of a difficult life out on the road and the poor wages of a bus driver.

With nerves jangling I was sent out on my first assignment to pick up a playgroup of mothers and small children. The pick-up point was in Byker, a suburb on the east side of Newcastle with a proud industrial past including being the home of Maling pottery. These days it is better known for Ralph Erskine's world renowned building, the Byker Wall, which was built in the 1970's, or for the children's TV programmes Byker Grove and The Stables.

I arrived in my 57-seater coach outside to find all the mothers standing on the pavement outside the community centre, rocking their pushchairs and skilfully juggling their duties of feeding their babies and holding on to their toddlers while smoking a cigarette. They were off for a picnic at a beauty spot near Bedlington called Plessey Woods, no more than twenty minutes drive.

It all went swimmingly until we turned off the main road and started going down a steep hill on a road which abruptly narrowed until it became little more than a farm track. The mothers were adamant that they had been down this road before in a bus. Soon I had passed the point of no return and could only inch the bus down between two hefty dry stone walls on a hairpin bend. We made it; by the skin of our teeth into a larger car park at the bottom next to the river.

While the group had their barbecue picnic, I went to examine the possibility of how I was going to get out of this damp and midge infested spot. The sky darkened and the trees came alive with the sounds of cawing rooks near the bad corner I was going to have to negotiate. I am occasionally superstitious and took the sudden arrival of the crows to be a bad omen.

The signs were exactly right and when it was time to leave, I got well and truly stuck. The group's appalling set of directions and my inexperience of driving buses was the precursor for disaster. How the hell was I going to drive this big bus around the tight corner?

It got worse. The already nervous passengers became panic stricken and near hysterical when the wheels started slipping and smoking on the wet bend. The smell of burning rubber and the sounds of grinding metal on stone, as I collided with the wall, was more than they could bear. The screaming from the children and many of the mothers aggravated the nightmare. They demanded to be let off the bus. I opened the door, but there was more screaming as the door slammed against the wall with a bang and paintwork scattered on the wet verge. They squeezed through the narrow gap and ran to safety.

The group waited under a tree at the top of the hill, sheltering from the rain and glaring at me as I tried to get the empty bus out of this mess. It was misery personified. Following some more screeching and grinding as the wheel trim became detached, the bus finally emerged into the wider part of the track relatively unscathed, given the circumstances. There were a few dents, in addition to the removed wheel trim, which the fitters should be able to beat out. I did not want to get a reputation like another driver who I heard the mechanics discussing earlier that day, "How is she doing?" one had asked.

"Fine," replied the other, "she's keeping the panel beaters busy."

As I reached the top of the hill, the atmosphere changed. The unpleasant noises were replaced with children whooping and cheering. I looked in the mirror to see the organiser walking behind the bus, holding the mangled wheel-trim. I felt a sigh of relief. I checked again and asked the mothers if they were sure that they had had been down that road before in a bus.

"Yes, but no, maybe" they replied sheepishly. "Come to think of it – I think we went in ... mini-buses."

Back at the depot, the boss was not too pleased about his third smartest bus being dented. His misplaced confidence in his newest driver had ebbed away, when I reported that I had crashed on my very first day. It can only have been an act of Hobson's choice to let me loose with the pride of the fleet, a smart Mercedes coach 24 hours later. It had a quirky computerised gearbox, which only needed fingertip touch to change gear. The computer was sensitive and temperamental due mainly to being overridden by rough drivers. They would try to drive it like an ordinary bus and ram it into gear, which resulted in the computer first of all going into a sulk and stuttering through the gears it decided to use, then giving up completely and refusing to co-operate at all. As a consequence the bus was a frequent visitor to the Mercedes main dealer. The fitters at the depot were flummoxed by the complexity of it.

But for the shortage of drivers I would never have been allowed within striking distance of the front door lever. There was no luxury of picking and choosing, so I was sent with another more experienced driver to double drive the Newcastle to London National Express run. It went smoothly until we arrived back at the terminus in Newcastle. Gallowgate Bus Station was an aesthetically pleasing 1930s building with its distinctive windows and huge sliding doors of the garage and inspection pit tacked on to the side. The curved design and railings on both upper and lower floors made it look like an Art Deco concrete battleship. It could and should have been preserved as a monument to the early history of bus travel in Britain, but it was demolished to make way for two new faceless office blocks.

Arriving back at the deserted, old bus station after midnight presented problems to inexperienced drivers like myself. Tiredness and poor lighting made it difficult to see what was behind when reversing into the coach bay. The reflection of the orange sodium streetlights from the adjacent street in the puddles made it even more confusing. I promptly reversed the Mercedes into the concrete awning and left two dents by the rear window. The London passengers woke up with a jolt. Welcome to Newcastle.

The loud bang was enough to wake up the wino lying on the bench. The green and silver paint marks from the Mercedes were clearly visible on the white awning until the bus station was torn down. Thereafter every time I walked past with my children they would become animated and point at the roof with the missing concrete and say, "Daddy did that!"

National Express, was nicknamed National Distress or Nasty Express by the other drivers who worked on the routes. It was stressful work for the full time drivers and many scowled when it was put on to their duty roster. But I always used to find it interesting work, undoubtedly because I was not a full time driver and the novelty of journeying to different cities had not worn off yet. The bus company ran a duplicate service when the National Express main service coaches were overbooked.

At peak times and bank holidays National Express would have to subcontract whichever company they could get hold of. This usually meant an assortment of older buses would be on hand. There was a rush of passengers for the lead bus when they noticed our rickety old coach parked behind it. You could feel the disappointment when passengers who were told that the main service coach was full were directed on to the overflow coach. They knew that the gleaming white coach with red, white and blue National Express logo emblazoned on its sides would have smart uniformed drivers, a pleasant hostess selling food and hot drinks and more legroom.

On our coach there were two rough and ready drivers, 57 cramped seats, often with chewing gum stuck under the armrests as it had been on the school run the previous day, no food and tepid water from the boiler added to a spoon of mellow instant coffee and some 'powdered cow' (whitener), served by a driver who more often than not swayed in the aisle and spilt it. No wonder there was a stampede for the other coach.

Victoria Coach Station was an extraordinary place where many varieties of life converged and dispersed. It was a rambling building which stank of stale chips and cheap cooking fat, 24 hours a day. The smelly sock and trainers brigade were flopped across the plastic seats, snoring loudly with their footwear removed. Many wore odd socks of varying shades of mustard colour. It seemed to be their uniform for a backpacking trip on the buses.

The corridors bustled with people of all sizes, some on the larger side who pushed past in a terrible hurry. The suitcases were large as were the lumbering, steel-framed backpacks. The Eastern Europeans often seemed to have brought the entire contents of their kitchens, as a result there was frequently the sound of clanging metal as they squeezed past each other. Tempers often flared and the behaviour of some on the concourse resembled that of cattle being sent into the sale ring at the mart.

An entertaining pastime for drivers was to spot the many people who had been soaked to the skin, even when there was a cloudless sky. These were the people who tried to take an illegal shortcut into the coach station, through the shed where arriving buses dropped off their passengers. Little did they realise that, at the entrance, there were sprinklers and when a bus went past a certain point it would trigger a sensor. A gentle yet persistent spray of water would be deployed to keep the dust levels down. Unfortunately a person walking through this entrance would equally well trigger the sensor and this resulted in a free shower.

Victoria Coach Station was a hospitable place for bus drivers. There was no need to go anywhere near the public area as there were plenty of facilities exclusively for drivers and hostesses. There was a drivers' café where everyone used to meet. The room was bubbling with chit chat. It was a haven following the previous hours of boredom on motorways or fighting through London traffic and road rage. The canteen served solid food and it was where the hostesses replenished their supplies, buying wholesale from the caterer and reselling on the coach. One of the drivers I regularly went with had the place sussed. He had even managed to find out the four digit numerical code for the executives' lavatories, so we would sneak through the door and up the stairs and spend our time out in great comfort.

But best of all were the foreign buses and spending time with their crews. The German buses were immaculate and the newest makes. They often had an upturned schnapps bottle and paper cups by the door for any returning passenger who needed it. The Polish buses were dilapidated old knackers which would not have been out of place in on some road through the Atlas Mountains, as they seemed to have a permanent list due to faulty suspension. Onboard there was always a party going on. Half an hour before they were due to leave the drivers and the hostesses would be sitting round a table on the bus with ties loosened, sleeves rolled up, drinking vodka and eating Polish sausages.

This was the new transition period from communism to capitalism and it was going to take some time yet before they received new buses.

The National Express Hostesses were professional, hard working and fun. They brought style to an otherwise unglamorous form of transport. They were unfairly viewed as the poor relation to the air hostess (though some went on to work for the airlines), going to mundane destinations, serving sandwiches and teas and coffees a to steerage class clientele. They suffered most by having to wear a very dowdy looking uniform which they complained about and said they felt that it gave them a frumpy image. They were amazingly tolerant of disparaging songs about them from groups such as *The Divine Comedy*. The lyrics from *National Express* made you wonder why they continued in the job:

> On the National Express there's a jolly hostess
> Selling crisps and tea
> She'll provide you with drinks and theatrical winks
> For a high-sky fee
> Mini-Skirts were in style as she danced down the aisle
> Back in '63 (yeah, yeah, yeah, yeah)
> But it's hard to get by when your arse is the size
> Of a small country

There was one hostess who took great exception and used to vociferously challenge the authenticity of the lyrics. Any passenger humming the tune would be evicted from her bus. She happened to be very good looking and therefore always had an entourage of drivers around her who hung on her every word. She did not mind what she said. When her fluttering eyelashes weren't working overtime with the drivers, she would give a commentary of all the passengers who were about to board and the nickname she gave each city they were going to.

"Yes, well we seem to have a full payload today. We have...

"20 Miserable Buggers (MIDDLESBOROUGH)"
"10 Corn Merchants (STOCKTON-ON-TEES)"
"3 Oat Eaters- (Quakers Oats) (DARLINGTON)"
"4 Klingons (HARTLEPOOL)"
"5 Macems (SUNDERLAND)"
"5 Sand Dancers (SOUTH SHIELDS)"
"3 Geordies (NEWCASTLE)"
"2 Geordies Who Can Swim (NORTH SHIELDS)"

The passengers who boarded the bus seemed to ignore the fact that they were being made fools of. It was the antidote to the boredom of the job and the complaining nature of members of the general public.

Accidents were rare. A driver allegedly once took a corner too fast. It was ironic as witnesses thought he was making a safety announcement to the passengers at the time. There was another crash, years ago which resulted in some fatalities, including a hostess. The damaged coach was supposedly taken away, discreetly repaired and then put back on the road under a new identity. Strange and eerie things began to happen and the many hostesses refused to travel on this particular bus, even though they knew nothing of its past history. Some said they felt as if there was someone following them, like a spirit. The gossip soon became rife that many people began to think it must be the ghost of the hostess who had been killed in the crash and the bus was haunted.

Some drivers detested the job as they felt as if they were being exploited and worked to the bone. On the job sheet it might have looked straightforward, entailing a simple Newcastle-London return, which would mean being back home before midnight. On arrival at Victoria, the dispatcher was quite likely to ask you to take a bus down to Bristol or Canterbury or Southampton and back, or stay the night, before going home to Newcastle, possibly via somewhere like Manchester or Liverpool, depending on the number of driving hours you still had left. The European Directives would be stretched to the limit. Sometimes you would run out of hours completely and be stranded in Devon or Cornwall. So the days were long and you never knew where you might end up. The old hands always packed an overnight bag – just in case.

On Saturdays in the summer there was a scheduled service from Newcastle to Great Yarmouth. This was like a time warp as the passengers were rarely under 80 and each year there were fewer and fewer. It was a similar tradition to Scots' Week in Whitley Bay where historically after the Glasgow Fair the Glaswegians would descend on this seaside town for their holidays. Some Geordies seemed to like going for their seaside holidays in Yarmouth and didn't mind the 6-hour drive.

How enjoyable the day was depended heavily on who was assigned as your driving partner. As in all double drives, it was a lottery. Most drivers wanted to avoid being paired with colleagues such as the nervous Barton or Jumpy Joe, who would arrive at work smelling of alcohol and had a habit of revving the engine so hard that he destroyed many clutches and gearboxes. He also had a reputation of blowing up engines by neglecting to put any water in them.

Barton's nerves were unpredictable that he would sometimes lose it altogether and simply walk off. Once, one of the most experienced drivers accompanied him on a National Express job from Newcastle to London Victoria. Having got some way down the A1 with no more stops to make, he put Barton into the driver's seat and feeling fairly sure nothing could go wrong, he retired to the back of the bus for a sleep. When he woke up he had an uneasy feeling and the passengers were muttering under their breath, which was always a bad sign. He looked out of the window and saw signs that said M1 The North – Leeds 4 miles.

'Bloody hell,' yelled the experienced driver as he leapt out of his seat. Barton had experienced a panic attack and somehow taken a northbound route on to a completely different motorway. The service that day had arrived in London about 5 hours later than scheduled. Road-works and an enforced detour were the official reasons given for the delay, which failed to pacify the passengers, who were quick to demand refunds for the 200-mile detour.

Barton could have an attack of nerves at any time. When it happened, he could drive no further. On a service route once through a part of Wearside, some baseball-capped youths physically punched the side of the bus in a fit of anger. They hit it so hard that there were knuckle marks on every panel. Barton was found shaking in the driver's seat of his bus, which was stationary in the middle of the road at a busy junction. He was a gibbering wreck. It did not take long for him to do a vanishing act.

"He's like an Aborigine," said the boss. "He just goes bloody walk-about." This time disappeared and could not be found for weeks. The shortage of drivers had now become so critical, that the boss trawled the streets looking for him. He would never find him, but Barton would always turn up out of the blue, in his own time, drive for another few days or weeks, before disappearing again.

Though the high turnover of drivers was common throughout the bus industry, it seemed to be particularly bad at this company. Pay and stress were the reasons combined with alleged rumours of cash-flow problems and a company teetering on the brink. The wages were low and the older drivers would reminisce about the days when the North Eastern bus driver was once the highest paid bus driver in the country before de-regulation of the industry in 1986.

The more experienced drivers who had being doing the job for a long time often acted like old soldiers. One called Lex used to play the system for all it was worth, especially when he arrived at a service station on the motorway. Granada (as it was then) gave a loyalty card to coach drivers and whenever they brought a coach load into one of their service stations, the card would be swiped and points would be attributed which would be converted into cash at the end of the year. Lex, whose normal pace was leisurely would, without warning break into an ungainly sprint and race over the bridge to the other services on the opposite carriageway so that he could have his card swiped again and get double points. The service station companies have since tightened up on the rules.

Another driver called Damien thought a great deal about himself and liked to consider himself as the top driver. He used to advertise this fact to his passengers at every opportunity.

"I'm Damien ... I'm the company's No.1 driver."

There was sometimes a sign above the driver's seat in almost similar words which would reinforce this statement. His balloon was pricked however, on a trip to France as he journeyed across the sands to Mont Saint Michel. For some reason he veered off the causeway and the bus sank rapidly in the quicksand. It made the national news in France and some of the British papers. The French media had a field day and tended to portray him as an idiotic 'ros bif' driver. The passengers were not amused either as their expensive holiday was brought to a halt.

"If you are the number one driver," snarled an angry lady, "I hate to think what the others are like?"

The boss spat venom and could hardly speak to Damien for weeks. Apart from the humiliation and embarrassment of his company being ridiculed internationally, there was the financial equation where a very large and very expensive crane had to be hired to pull the bus out. Any profit from the excursion vanished.

The main body of the bus company's business was service work. This was mainly dull work with the odd flashes of excitement and covered many areas of varying demographics. It was a good way to learn the geography of the region.

Many of the events around the buses in the cities of the North East are probably only slightly different to other parts of the country. The early part of the evening driving in somewhere like Sunderland would sometimes be spent watching cars being chased by police at full speed. Some of the route passed through areas which were favoured short cuts used by getaway cars. The last run would always be the trickiest. There was often fighting in the central bus station, with drunks trying to catch the last bus home. Young children would be out roaming the streets and liked to play chicken with the oncoming buses. Gangs of hoodie-clad youths would stand in the middle of the road making obscene gestures at the bus drivers, or any driver for that matter. Sometimes they became belligerent and refused to move. It was the best policy to be patient and try to ignore them as they were looking for the slightest excuse to do some damage. I felt vulnerable as the mobile phones we carried were not the most reliable. Mostly they would get bored and finally wander off.

There was one little boy who lived in a house with a head on view of the road. I would pass directly under his window and learnt to look for the slightest waver in the drawn curtains. If there was I would take pre-emptive action and cover my eyes because the boy would without warning leap out and shine a laser torch in my eyes. A strong strip of red light would temporarily blind me and my eyes would be sore for the rest of the night. He must have moved, because I noticed the patterns on the curtains had changed from footballs to princesses. There were never any problems again.

Having been zapped, it was a relief to turn right up the hill, to the top and pull up outside the Working Men's Club. The doors would open and an army of well-oiled, elderly men, women and couples ascended the bus steps. The bus would start to sway gently. The more that got on, the more the gentle swaying turned to violent rocking. These were well built passengers who had just endured a lengthy session at the Club. They were in a jovial mood. Bright red in the face and full of slurred chitter chatter, the suspension of the bus lowered so much that you could hear the wheels rubbing against the wheel arches. It was an effort and the poor old bus struggled manfully up the first hill, emitting clouds of black smoke in protest as she went.

The atmosphere and strong smell of alcohol inside the bus must have been similar to a bootleg gin palace. I used to feel quite light headed from breathing in all the fumes. But there was never any kind of trouble. A new bus driver quickly learnt that there were certain principles that had to be adhered to. Rule No.1: the passengers expected a reduced fare ride home. They never paid the full amount, but would put 50p or whatever change they had in their pockets. This was given to the bus driver and not expected to go into the takings along with the other fares. An inspector once heard about these antics and tried to board the bus to check tickets and recoup some of the lost revenue, but he was bodily removed and dumped on the pavement. I never saw another inspector and it was likely that they were fearful for their lives.

The club members tried through the alcoholic haze to make small talk and ask the usual question.

"You're not from round here are you?"

There were the usual background sounds of a simultaneous combination of escaping wind and hiccups, punctuated with sudden shouts from the back of "Next stop, driver!" Invariably the ones who wanted to get off first would always be at the back of the bus. The swaying would continue until two perspiring beings appeared from beneath the armpit of someone who was holding on to the straps hanging down from the roof. The veterans of the bus never held on as they knew it was packed so tightly that there was never any danger of anyone falling over.

Gradually the suspension returned to normality and the swaying ceased as more disembarked. The final person to leave the bus was the largest, smartest and the most drunk. He was always immaculately dressed in a dark suit and tie. He had the physical shape of Oliver Hardy and also similar mannerisms and general appearance. Rumour had it that he was a respected craftsman called Clarence, who would slowly manoeuvre himself down the bus. As he reached the driver he would feel into his pocket, jangle a great mass of coins and in a slurred voice say: "Driver, I want to give you something."

The first time this happened, I felt an air of anticipation. Was this Father Christmas coming early? Would it be a £5 note, or a £1 coin or a 50p bit? After a great deal of rummaging he took something out of his pocket and placed it on the cash tray. He then bade goodnight, managed with difficulty to negotiate the steps and wended a slow and tortuous route towards his house. I drove off, stopping round the next corner so that I could see what wonderful tip had been left.

It was 5p. A measly 5p bit.

I started to laugh. The bus was empty, so I could make as much noise as I liked. After the initial feeling that I was the victim of a hoax I changed my mind the next time I drove that route when exactly the same thing happened. Clarence, it turned out, travelled on that bus every night. Every night he tipped the driver 5p. That amounted to over £18 a year (if you discount Christmas Day and Easter Day when the bus didn't run). Though he saved about £218.40 in unpaid fares which made the tip seem a bargain.

The other route I used to drive in Sunderland was around Pennywell, a suburb which had a reputation then for being notoriously rough and was considered one of the worst estates in the North East. The newspapers carried stories of stabbings and all sorts of anti-social behaviour. Many houses were boarded up and the roads and pavements were littered with broken glass from the bottles that had been flung the previous evening. In amongst the broken glass there were marks which looked suspiciously like blood stains.

I had the misfortune to break down early one morning. Leaving the bus was a risk and I feared returning to find something missing, or to find a pile of bricks where the wheels had once been. The only help available was from a security guard in a closed supermarket who reluctantly came out of his safe cubicle. The shop's twenty-four hour security consisted of alarms, security cameras and winding strings of razor wire as well as a roster of guards. From there I called for a replacement bus. I need not have worried about vandalism or being mugged as it was a Sunday morning and everyone was sleeping off the effects of the night before.

A sometimes comparable experience was driving the Benwell Hoppa, a circular bus route which toured an area on the West side of Newcastle, with an equally poor reputation. It did not inspire confidence when you passed the vacated, fire damaged, old church and seeing the odd youth hiding behind a hedge, looking shifty. But fortunately most of the passengers were elderly and were so weighed down by shopping that nothing bad ever happened. Some of the pensioners had what I considered to be low aspirations as their afternoon entertainment seemed to consist of doing three consecutive circuits before getting off, saying, "Thank you, driver, that was a very nice journey." I think they saw the Hoppa as a cheap coach trip.

There was another service which was known as the "Jarvis Contract". It sounded like a Cold War spy novel, but was most likely named after the company which sponsored the route. It involved taking students from Wearside and Tyneside to a college in North Northumberland. The route started in Sunderland, went along the south side of the Tyne, through Jarrow, Hebburn and Heworth, into Gateshead and Newcastle City Centre before heading out on the north side of the Tyne through Byker and

North Shields before going up towards Cramlington and Ashington.

On the return journey the fiery youths would huddle together at the back. There would be the sound of coins being thrown into a bag. At first I thought they were gambling and playing poker, but they were hurriedly scrabbling in their pockets and throwing whatever change they had into a bag. One of them came to the front, dumped the bag on the dashboard and grunted into my ear, "Er, Mister, here's the money to pay the Tyne Tunnel toll and we were wondering if you could take the short cut so that we could get home earlier."

It was technically illegal to deviate off the prescribed route and could have resulted in the bus company losing the contract. But all drivers did it. It made for a peaceful journey and, besides, if the boss ever queried it, the standard excuse was that it was saving the company money on diesel.

It all came to a head when some of the youths went too far and started smoking joints in the back of the bus. The police were tipped off by someone within the company and one afternoon, when the bus was emerging from the Tyne Tunnel, it was ushered into a lay-by where a police car was waiting. As the bus stopped and the driver opened the front doors to let the policemen on, there was frantic activity at the back of the bus. The emergency exit door was flung open and a variety of items and substances were thrown over the adjacent hedge. The policemen did not notice this. When they searched them, they protested their innocence and complained of police harassment. The bus had a lingering smell of cannabis smoke for days afterwards.

One of the routes I drove the most was in South Shields. This was supposed to be one of the most valuable contracts then in the North East. The boss had managed to win it, much to the annoyance of the larger bus companies. It was a route that twisted and turned its way through an unusual town, which was half seaside resort and half industrial commuter town and a working port. It was also a coalmining area, where much of its industrial heritage and past were still visible.

The route carried a gentle stream of passengers. It was rarely busy. At night time it quietened down and became, at times, morose. One night, with little else to do, I started to count the landmarks and points of interest along the route. On a 20-minute journey between Harton Moor Estate and The Lawe Top, which overlooked the mouth of the Tyne and the sea I passed:

47 Pubs
49 Take-Aways (20 Indian and Bangladeshi, 10 Chinese, 10 Fish 'n Chips, 7 Italian, a Kebab House, a Vegetarian)
18 Hairdressers
3 Factories
3 Metro Stations
2 Oil Rigs (being repaired at McNulty's yard on the Tyne)
2 Lighthouses
1 Town Hall
1 Benefits Office
1 Hospital
1 Port
1 Pleasure Beach
1 Model Railway
1 Ocean Going Sea Ferry
and numerous Tanning Salons

There can be few bus routes so diverse, in such a short space of time. Russian ships would dock at the Port of Tyne and the sailors' wives would be allowed into the town to go shopping. When these ladies were standing in the bus stops, wearing long black shawls and traditional brown or black linen dresses with white floral embroidery, I knew that there was a Russian ship docked in the port. They would appear at any bus stop, looking lost and miserable, always holding a scrunched up piece of paper in their hands with "Port of Tyne" written on it. They spoke no English and their eyes pleaded with the bus driver to take them back to their ship, free of charge.

I was considered a madman by the other drivers when I used to bring my swimming trunks with me, and go for a dip in the sea during my rest period in the summertime. There was never much time, but I managed to time it to perfection on hot days, fitting in a swim, an ice cream and a cappuccino in forty-five minutes. Sometimes the sea would be so inviting that I cut it fine and got back on to the bus, dripping sea water over the passengers. Swimming restored my sanity and it always made the next five and a half hour shift go quicker.

The boss was struggling to keep the bus route going. This was partly due to the increasing unreliability of his drivers who he never knew for sure whether they would turn up or not. Gradually the complaints rose that buses were running early, late or not at all. He received warnings from the Passenger Transport Authority and was called more and more to their offices to explain the poor performance.

His latest habit of sitting in his car in the North Shields car park, on the other side of the river, peering through his binoculars to surreptitiously check that the bus was not running early, was soon twigged by the drivers who did not take kindly to being spied on. This created an air of distrust and employer relations hit rock bottom. It was a vicious circle and the result was that he struggled even more for reliable drivers. Rumours bounced round about the company's financial health and even including one about whether one of the managers was having a dalliance with another's wife or not.

Things did not seem to be going well. The first visible confirmation was when the accountant was seen running across the car park with a briefcase, allegedly full of the day's takings, being hotly pursued by a manager who spreadeagled him with the textbook rugby tackle. The case flew open, releasing the contents on to the tarmac and coins rolled in every direction, some finding the drain. No one knew the true reason why the accountant acted in the way he did, but the drivers believed that he may have seen that company was about to cease trading, and thought that he had better take what was owed to him in fees while he still could.

The last misfortune to befall me, before I left the company came when my car, or to be precise the Subaru Justy I borrowed from my mother was stolen from outside the front door of the depot. I've always believed bad things happen in threes. I'd walked into the bathroom door first thing and later I had seen two double-deckers collide in Sunderland Central Bus Station. They had demolished the council's ornate railings, but amazingly no one had been hurt. One of the drivers said that his accelerator had jammed giving him no control. He had shut his eyes and prayed hard as he headed towards the other bus.

A good rule I have discovered in the bus world, is never to laugh at the errors or misfortunes of another driver because it always came back to haunt you. I had been thinking about the double-decker driver's excuse and if it was the truth or a lie, when I failed to look properly in my mirror and reversed my bus into the back of another outside the depot, in full view of the mechanics. This was a second bad thing to happen to me and I should have been watching out for the third.

I was tired when I finished my shift and keen to get home so I went out to the car park, turned the ignition key in the Justy and left it to warm the engine up. There was another driver sitting in his car parked next door, who said he would watch it until I returned from running an errand to another driver in the depot.

As I was speaking to Syd the driver, we both heard the high pitched revving noise and screeching of tyres coming from outside An uncomfortable feeling hit the base of my stomach and I rushed out of the depot to see the Justy being driven at high speed in reverse by a stranger in a baseball cap. Smoke was emanating from the tyres. The stench of burnt rubber hung in the air. Needless to say the 'reliable' driver who had said he would watch over the car was nowhere to be seen.

Syd, who was a part-time bus driver took decisive action, told me to jump into his motor and, together we would chase the thief. His main business was running his own garage, so our pursuit vehicle was not a car but a bashed up blue Ford van, emblazoned with the logo on both sides:

SYD'S GARAGE
CONCEPT 2000

As the Justy disappeared I thought that was the last I was going to see of it. Syd, however told me to have patience and that we should look around the area for a little while. He was right because after no more than five minutes, the Justy came shooting out of a side street. We were right behind it. We were catching up with the Justy. At one point we nearly overtook it. The springs were not so hot on Syd's van and every time we hit a bump, I rose up and hit my head on the ceiling. I did not notice as the adrenaline was rushing so hard, but as I looked at myself in the mirror the next day, I had a bruise on the top of my forehead. Syd handed me his mobile phone and I was soon talking to 999 where a strange conversation took place:

"Emergency Services – can I help you?"

"Yes, yes, quick," I must have said in extremely panicked tones, "I've had my car stolen and we are following it in Syd's van and we are going round the roundabout at somewhere on the south side of the Tyne. Quick! Quick! Call the police."

"Oh I am sorry, dear, I can't do that, there is a five minute delay before we can connect you to the police."

"You can't be serious, please hurry, we're now right behind him, he's going towards the motorway, up the bank ... no, no, he's turned back to the roundabout, now he's turned off and is going into a pub car park behind the pub and now the other bar ... quick, quick!"

In the background Syd was shouting in excitement: "Now we've got the bastard – it's a dead end!"

Sure enough it was a dead end and the thief tried to turn around and ran directly into the headlights of Syd's van. For a second he looked like a startled rabbit.

"He's stopped, he's getting out ... oh shit ... he's got a gun..."

Syd and I, though fired up, could not be described as the bravest. We put our arms over our heads and ducked. I ended up examining the dirt and accumulated rubbish in the footwell of Syd's van, whilst hearing gunfire outside, wondering whether my last view of the world would be of a scrunched up can of Coke.

BANG, BANG, BANG.

I still had the phone glued to my ear and could hear the rather more urgent tones of the 999 Operator.

"Are you still there, dear? We heard what sounded like shots."

I grabbed the phone and replied in a voice which must have been far too squeaky to be good.

"Yes, f---ing hell, yes, call the police, someone is shooting at us."

I remembered thinking that Syd's van was so full of rusty holes, another few bullet holes wouldn't matter a great deal. The good sign was that, though there were the shots, there was no sound of any bullets hitting anything. There were no pinging noises or ricochets. There was hope.

"Well, dear now that we have heard shooting we have reported the incident to the nearest police units and they should be with you shortly."

Shortly? Oh, yeah, I thought, I've heard that one before.

But she was right. Within 45 seconds all hell broke loose. There were police cars, police vans, police dog vans, with slobbering snarling Alsatians, an armed response unit and a helicopter circling overhead with an intense spotlight trained on the ground. The police had done well to find us considering the useless drivel I was directing to the 999 operator and subsequent delay.

The thief had headed for the undergrowth and was never seen again. Amazingly the Justy was still in one piece, externally at least. Internally it was a different story. It soon became apparent I had a good deal of explaining to do to my mother. It was difficult to figure out a gentle way of breaking the news that the car only needed a new clutch, gearbox, exhaust and brake system. It was never the same car again and a few months later, even with its major repair work, was to become a recruit at a Tyneside breakers yard.

The arrival of what seemed to be the complete resources of the Tyneside Constabulary had coincided with a phone call from the publican of one of the pubs who had been on his way to bed and was drawing the curtains. He had heard the shots, looked down into the car park and on seeing a man firing a gun, had dialled 999. The next two hours were spent in the back of a police car, going over the crime scene with two policemen.

By the time I was allowed to go, it was well after midnight. I was tired, hungry and in a black mood.

I left the dark and dingy bus company depot and was momentarily deceived by the peacefulness in the night air. Only hours earlier it had it been a so much more violent place. It was the last time I went there as soon after the company went into liquidation.

It was time to move on. I had completed my first job in the bus industry and now had no fear about the line which regularly appeared in most job adverts which stated: 'Minimum 1 Year's experience.' I had enjoyed my time in Tyneside, but the commute to work was just short of the hour and it was debateable whether the wages did much more than cover the cost of the petrol.

It was now time to search closer to home. Living in the High Pennines in Northumberland posed its problems with most types of employment. It was unlikely there would be much activity in the bus industry.

There couldn't possibly be a bus company in such a remote rural area – or could there?

The Safeway free bus on the inspection pit in the depot was not an unusual occurrence.

This was my first bus depot. I reversed my bus into the bumper of another bus as the mechanic watched on.

Appleby Fair time was one of my favourite times of year. Here is a view from my bus of a travellers' camp.

Wembley Stadium coach park at the 1998 Championship Play-Off Final, Sunderland vs Charlton. Black Cats fans were full of optimism.

'What have you broken now, Tom?' This was the fitter's favourite question he always asked me.

'We've lost! It'll be a long trip back up North.'

CHAPTER 3

THE BUS COMPANY AT THE TOP OF THE HILL

Somewhere, high up in the Pennine hills, sits a bitter-sweet village. It is an old lead mining village which stands well above sea level, vying for the title of highest village in England. Though Flash in the Derbyshire Peak District officially holds the title, the village shop is undaunted and still sells postcards which proudly pronounce their village as the highest. It is inhabited by an eclectic local community, gaining a reputation as a destination for hippies and new age travellers, who mainly arrived there in the late 1960s and early 1970s. They sought an alternative and utopian way of living in this wet and windy valley. The derelict houses were relatively cheap then and it was out of the way.

Drugs were sometimes an issue, not aided by the fact that it was the perfect habitat for wild magic mushrooms to grow. The well banded about local joke was that if cannabis was ever legalised, attics in various houses in the region would revert to their normal use.

In the 1980s the village became synonymous with large outdoor music festivals, a sort of Northern version of Glastonbury, but with clouds of midges. The owners of a farm organised the event and gave the event a lunar name. At first it was a great success, attracting well-known bands. The catering consisted of a chip fryer in the barn producing veggie burgers and chips. Most, if not all of the food was vegetarian. There were craft stalls and a scrumpy van came up from the West Country.

Everyone brought their tents and camped. Over time the festival attracted the attention of the police who parked on the main road and took photographs of the festival goers as they came and went. Mug shots began to be posted on a billboard in the local police station. The festival eventually ceased.

The area was heavily industrialised with the mining of lead other minerals and the surrounding countryside was still littered with mine shafts, slag heaps and other tell-tale signs of the area's industrial past.

The village was also interesting for its Quaker connections. Throughout the last three centuries philanthropy has been evident none more so than when two women were travelling through the area at the end of the 17th Century. They were so concerned about the conditions the miners and their families were living under that they decided to do something about it. It became the site for a new model village. Houses were built, together with Sunday Schools, gardens, a chapel, a clock tower and a market hall. Trees were planted and agriculture was encouraged. In the mid 19th Century, the Quakers built a house for the vicar, a post office, a water supply and a public wash house. Everything was based around the premise that good health made for a contented workforce and a happy life. They also provided a lending library for the miners, and when trade diminished at the local pub, it was observed that the miners preferred reading to drinking.

The population has decreased from the many thousands, to the present day hundreds, and it was not until the bottom dropped out of the lead market that the Quaker Company folded in 1905. Various forms of mining continued under the new owners, but it was generally on the wane.

In the 1970s, groups of poets, writers and artists seemed to choose the Pennine hills as the perfect place to live a bohemian lifestyle, with a type of freedom which was quite unlike anywhere else.

Chapter 3

In the late 1990s the property boom brought a different group of people to the area as it became a sought after place to live. Many of the farms and byres were modernised and converted. More young families arrived.

The climate was harsh and unforgiving. The grey-black of the slag heaps was replicated by the grey-black mist and clouds which often enveloped the area and the grey-black stone and brick of the mainly terraced housing. The pub was the focal point of the village, next to the redundant chapel and temperance hall. It was the sort of pub where the seated drinkers at the bar, maintained their silence as they turned slowly and stared at the person who had come through the main entrance. On the other side of the road there was a windy playground where children hurtled across the zip wire.

Next to this was where I found the unlikely sight of a bus company depot in a redundant lead mining building.

It had been delivered, second hand from the Ruhr Valley in Germany, in the early 1900s to be used as a lead washing plant. The dowdy red brick and rusty metal struts ensured it bore a certain likeness to the Volgograd Tractor Factory in Stalingrad. The land upon which it stood, was polluted with lead spoilings. It was in desperate need of demolition and re-development but various requests had been met with indifference from various bodies.

The company who owned it were a respected bus operator and had been in business since the 1920s. They started by operating a service between the village and the local town in a pony and trap, during the First World War. They progressed to a Model T Ford and gradually bought larger and larger buses.

I found them quite by chance and decided to cold call to see if there was any kind of vacancy. I approached the large garage doors with trepidation, for fear of what may have lurked behind them in this imposing building. There was no one around. Some ageing Bedford buses were dwarfed in the vast space. The only consoling feeling was listening to the cacophony of sound coming from twittering sparrows who flew in and out of the holes in the roof and seemed most at home. I turned to the left, past the antique Gilbarco diesel pumps which registered gallons rather than litres and the main fuel tank which looked suspiciously like a 1930s tanker with the wheels removed and set into concrete. I pushed open the door which hopefully would lead to the office. It was not the office, but the drivers' lavatory.

There was no ceiling to this cubicle and when I looked upwards the birds were looking down from the rafters. It was to be my first encounter with what can only be viewed as avian humour as at that moment a sparrow flew past and a white blob landed on the crown of my head. It was followed shortly by another bird, who hit my shoulder.

As I emerged from the cubicle I noticed there was a shabby old Portakabin. The door opened and a man stared at me suspiciously. It turned out to be one of the directors. He seemed surprised that someone wearing a jacket and tie should be stumbling around the depot. "I want to learn about buses and tours," I stuttered nervously, "can you help?"

And so it was, I started out that very afternoon in an aged Bedford bus which had come off the factory assembly line in 1974 on the local school run. It was a sharp learning curve reversing into a ridiculously small school yard, through parked cars and dustbins. I held on to the steering wheel tightly, pressed hard on the flabby brake pedal down the town's steep, cobbled, main street, continued through the narrow country lanes and just avoided contact with a tight, right angled stone bridge. The schoolchildren viewed me with suspicion as they were unused to seeing a driver in a tweed jacket and tie. When

I returned to the depot in one piece, I felt like a champion. It felt good.

The air in the village must have contained something life-enhancing, because many of the other drivers I met that afternoon were well over 70 years old. One was a farmer who was 79, one had driven trucks and buses all over the region, before he finally retired when he was 82 and another was 86, though on the verge of giving up. Many drivers had not taken their test until they were 59, seeing it as a good part-time retirement job.

The octogenarian had seen it all. He started driving buses in 1949, in the days when the snows came with a vengeance and when the company was known across the North of England by the phrase: 'Their buses will always get through.' Once, in the snow, he had driven the service bus over the tops of the hills and across the moors, through appalling weather conditions. Those days there were conductors on all buses who would take fares and pull the cord which rang a bell in the driver's cab and gave him the all clear to start off. On this occasion a passenger must have rung the bell because as he arrived at the destination, he suddenly noticed that there was no sign of the man anywhere on the vehicle. He jumped out of the bus and there, on the roof rack with all the luggage was the conductor, frozen stiff. When the bell had rung the driver had driven away with the wretched man still on the roof.

Another day when he was driving, a different conductor was concentrating on delivering the papers as the bus drove along the route, flinging the rolled up bundles out of the window into various drives and gateways. A car driver following behind thought the papers were accidentally falling off the bus and stopped to pick them up. At the terminus the conductor was presented with the pile of papers and in anger turned to him, shook her fist and blurted out: "Thou fool."

As in my first bus driving job it took time for me to stop making stupid mistakes. The first time I was on the college service bus I stalled 19 times between the depot and the college. How can I be so precise? It was because after each stall, all the students on the bus would in unison shout out the relevant number. After it reached double figures it became nauseating and embarrassing, destroying what little credibility and self-confidence I had as a proficient driver.

A lengthy school run was the next route. The school was over twenty miles away and the journey would take about one hour, with many stopping places. The students were feisty and, in one case, I took an instant dislike to one cantankerous individual who took pleasure in calling me 'son' in a cockily laboured voice. I kept my patience until after the umpteenth time he greeted me, when I felt something had to happen. It did and to my great satisfaction, whilst descending the steps when he got off, turned, deliberately chortled and said, "Goodbye son", overbalanced and fell headfirst into the mud. He never did it again and was soon to change schools.

The service from Tyneside to the Lake District was the jewel in the crown of the bus company. This route has been operating for close to 90 years and in its heyday, six buses would follow each other, in Indian file over the Pennines, with not one spare seat. It was a great tradition and all the passengers would disembark at a café for a half hour break.

The day was long. It meant leaving the depot at 7am and driving to Newcastle. The driver would have a twenty-minute break at Gallowgate Coach Station in a café which was mainly for National Express drivers and hostesses. It was a place to find out everything that was going on in the bus world. The dispatchers would appear sometimes and have a cup of tea in between making announcements on the loud speaker system and loading up the buses.

"How's National Express doing, these days?", I asked the veteran dispatcher.

"No different, man, it's never changed" he replied. "There are only four types who travel on National Express, students, grannies, ethnic minorities and the complete membership of the Jewish community."

I used to take a second cup of coffee back on to the bus where it would perch precariously on the plastic cash tray, which was one of the only level surfaces. The loading up process would take a long time, even if there were only a handful of passengers, because we had to handwrite every ticket, which were on triple carbonated papers. It took time to master the ancient ticketing system.

The trip took around 2½ hours to the Lakes. The passengers were often regulars and came back year after year, including a handful of what bus drivers affectionately call 'twirlies' or old aged pensioners. It stemmed from the whining, whinging tones of certain old folk when they missed their bus and would chastise the driver by saying:

"Bus driver. The bus – it's running too early."

The route across to the Lakes was one of the most stunning drives in England with spectacular views, when it was fine. It could also rain heavily and the bus would be immersed in low cloud and mist with the passengers being unable to see much out of the windows. The driver struggled to see out too, particularly when the demister on the bus could not cope with the extreme weather conditions. Sometimes it was a case of point and hope. The highlight of the journey would be as the bus climbed to 1900ft above sea level and rose over the crest of Hartside Top where there was a chance to overlook the Lake District, the Eden Valley and the Solway and see the Annan power station on the Dumfries coastline, twenty or thirty miles away.

It was a favourite road with bikers. The A686 had been voted the best road in England by one of the specialist motorbike magazines.

They came in droves, which made it hazardous driving a bus because as you descended and went round the hairpin bends, there was often an oncoming bike in the middle of the road. You looked into the whites of their eyes.

There was rumoured to be an unofficial race from a roundabout on the A69 to the café on the hill top. Each time they raced, the entry fee alledgedly went into a pot and fastest time of the year would scoop the pot. The pot would usually stand at around £5000 by the end of the season, so the racing took on a serious edge as it was not a prize to be sneezed at.

When the bus arrived in the Lakes there was a four-hour break until the return journey. I used to park, have a sleep, lunch and an amble round Keswick before getting ready for the return journey. Another part-time driver, Cockney Ron, who owned a pub would take the bus to the nearest cash and carry, anything up to 40 miles away. He would use the bus as a delivery van and stock up with supplies for the pub. The safe delivery of his supplies was far more important than the comfort of the passengers and he even forced a couple who were unwell to vacate their seats at the front "You can't bleeding well sit there. I need that seat for me tonic waters." The passengers meekly complied.

Cockney Ron never failed to surprise or amuse. On one trip he telephoned the boss very late having dropped off a group. "I'm in Richmond, what shall I do?" said Ron. "Oh good," replied the boss. "You'll be back soon – Yorkshire is only two hours from the depot."

"Nah not that Richmond, I'm in Richmond, Surrey."

"But we gave them a price to Richmond, Yorkshire, so tell them they have to pay a bit more."

"Nah – no chance! They've gone and I don't know where they

live." And so the company had to pick up the tab for this most unfortunate error.

He was famous within the company for getting the bus stuck in a narrow gateway, having decided to try the short cut and not take the usual route. He also managed to take a twelve metre bus over a bridge which other drivers struggled with eleven metre buses.

Ron sadly died a couple of years ago. His last request was that his coffin would go to his resting place on a bus. This was done, the bus was driven very slowly through the village to the graveyard, followed by the mourners. The logistics of placing the deceased Bob on the bus needed some careful planning as the coffin would not fit through the main door or the emergency exit.

It always reminded me of a similar operation which is supposed to have happened to a dead Polish General. He died in London during Communist times and was being flown back to Poland for a funeral with complete military honours. The placing of the coffin on to the LOT flight was left to a solitary ground handler at Heathrow Airport, who came up with an unusual solution to the problem of the Tupolev 134's narrow entry door. When the plane touched down at Warsaw, the band was playing and the communist leaders were saluting, but the guard of honour could not remove the coffin from the plane, try as they might.

At an enquiry into this embarrassment, it was found that the ground handler who was left on his own to put the coffin on the plane, could not get it through the narrow door either. So his solution was to lift up the lid, take out the deceased General and leave him propped up against the door. Then he dismantled the coffin and reassembled it in the First Class compartment of the plane, finally replacing the General and nailing down the lid.

Nothing this extreme happened to Ron. But the coffin had to be placed in the crew bunk where drivers can get some rest whilst on the move. The other drivers have since preferred to sit in the seat at the front while snoozing as no one wanted to go into the crew bunk ever again.

Back in Keswick, I found that the coach park in the Lake District town was a place where, time and again events were unpredictably theatrical. Anything seemed to happen in this parking area behind the main supermarket, where hordes of tourists were milling around and therefore it was impossible to avoid people watching. Buses came and went with regularity. There were drivers and passengers loitering around their buses, which meant there was nearly always a captive audience for any incoming buses. There was a temptation for the drivers to show off. They tended to come into the park at full speed, looking round to see who was watching, when they would stop concentrating and some proceeded to make fools of themselves.

A young, rather-too-pleased-with-himself driver, wearing faux Calvin Klein sunglasses zoomed majestically into the park, chewing gum and smoothing back his hair as he did so. He neglected to notice that one of the coach bays was shorter than the others because of a brick shed immediately behind it. He reversed as fast as he could, assuming that if he stopped with the front of his bus in line with the buses parked alongside then he need not use his mirrors to look behind him. As he reversed at full pelt he smiled at his audience.

CRASH!

He had demolished the wall. The rear end of his bus crumpled inwardly and the rear window disappeared altogether in a million fragments into the interior of the bus.

"That'll wipe the smile off his face," one of the watching drivers announced with glee.

I only ever saw one driver who did this safely, at speed and in style. She was a 6ft 2in. Amazonian blonde Dutch lady driver in a mini skirt. She arrived on a warm summer afternoon where every bizarre event happened in Keswick coach park that day. Having given a masterclass in coach driving, all the other drivers stood in a huddle and gawped as she descended the steps, then bowed in admiration of her skill. That was all except one, a very overweight and sweaty English driver, who had tried to sneak down the side of the bus for a crafty pee at the opposite end of the coach park without anybody noticing. He was firstly spotted by an embarrassed group of Morris Dancers who had come to find their bus. Then the Flying Dutch-lady walked past and loudly tut-tutted and whistled as she passed him. The driver hid behind his bus.

I was learning the tricks of the trade fast. The old teach the young both the good and the bad, but mainly the short cuts. Another driver showed me what to do with awkward passengers. Midway through a coach tour he put into action a carefully orchestrated campaign to end the tour early as he could no longer bear his moaning passengers and it seemed to be showing encouraging results. He would stop the bus in a high street outside a Woolworths store where there was a cardboard cut out figure of a shop assistant on the pavement outside the entrance. He would get out the bus, walk across the road and proceed to have a long conversation with this dummy as the increasingly perturbed passengers looked on. It was even better if there was a post box nearby, as he would look through the letter slot and, in a loud voice ask if the person inside the box was OK. The passengers were soon ringing the tour company demanding to go home.

Hearing these stories always gave me a false sense of invincibility and a feeling that I was a much more sensible driver who would never end up doing such nonsensical things. That was the time to watch out, but I never heeded the warning signs. So it was no surprise that when I left that day, I forgot to close the boot of the bus and all the rucksacks and luggage spilled out of the bus on to the road at the first turn out of the bus station. I could see the other drivers nodding their heads as if to confirm their satisfaction of seeing another deserving case get his comeuppance.

* * * * *

I was beginning to feel at home, driving for this new company. It was different from other bus companies. The two owners were thoroughly professional, but they also ran the place along relaxed lines and as if all their drivers and fitters were one big family. The company had been in business for a very long time and had a good name within the industry. Their geographical location meant they had to diversify and the drivers were an unusual mixture of farmers, ex-miners and an assortment of others oddballs such as myself. There were many part-timers. One who stood out was a 6' 8" giant was an ex-miner. I always considered myself tall, but he and his family towered above me. He had been with the bus company for over 30 years and was one of the few full time drivers.

The passengers adored him for his dry sense of humour and the many funny remarks which emanated from the driver's seat on most journeys. His motto was: "A happy bus is an empty bus". Any bus without moaning or aggressive passengers was a bonus in his eyes. Once an American lady failed to understand him when she asked him if the bus stopped in Heddon-on-the-Wall. "Yes, but only if someone gets off," he responded.

"Oh really? But that cannot be right" she said, looking mystified that British rural bus services could be quite so incompetent.

"What do you think this is? Public transport?" which silenced her as the rest of the passengers secretly laughed into their handkerchiefs.

Mervyn was well known for not taking any nonsense from other road users. A man and his wife were travelling in their car in the opposite direction through some urban conurbation, when there was an explosion of road rage. The man was shouting and swearing at him, and as he drew alongside the bus, he made a near fatal error of sticking two fingers up, out of the window. Mervyn leant out of the window and reached down into the man's car, grabbing him by the scruff of the neck and began to lift him out of his car through the drivers' wound down window. The man turned white with fear and his wife started shouting:

"I'm going to call the police!"

"Well you'd better be quick then," Mervyn told her, still holding her frightened husband who was now halfway out of his car and face to face with this angry bus driver, "and while you are at it you should ring for an ambulance at the same time!" This was the final straw. The man wriggled free, slammed his foot on the accelerator and disappeared around the corner.

All the drivers received nicknames from the bosses at the bus company. This was not hard as all the drivers exhibited peculiar mannerisms and were great characters. Dougal and Father Ted always did crass things. The Wolfman had a beard. Basil lived on top of a hill, had facial hair and kept goats, was soon known as Basil bin Laden. Crusty Flaps and Vinegar Jugs were grumpy female passengers. Hippy Harold was self explanatory.

The Pieman was so called because he ate his lunch in the driver's seat of a bus and always left a large amount of crumbs scattered around. He became even more famous and was splashed across the front page of the local paper for allegedly having spotted a large panther-like black cat rampaging around the moors. Though the beast has never been seen again, parallels were drawn with the tale of a wolf and reports of mass killings of sheep, which were reported up and down the valley in 1904. A year later a wolf was found dead on the railway tracks more than 30 miles away. No one was sure whether it was the same animal, but reports of livestock deaths fell and the wolf was never seen again.

The Pieman left the company and was the envy of all, as he became the highest paid bus driver in the county, driving the new 'Phone and Go' bus. Any member of the public could pick up the phone and request the mini-bus at anytime. The job was short lived and the service was a waste of time and money as mobile reception in the area was very poor. Few passengers ever phoned the bus. The Pieman sat in a field, on top of a hill, asleep on the back seat of the bus. It was one of the easiest jobs, but after a brief run, it was deemed to be unsustainable and quietly ditched. Someone later worked out that the running costs were so outrageous that a taxi ride in a stretch limo would have been a cheaper option.

Other drivers included Don, who was so laidback about everything. Nothing seemed to rile him except the attitude of the farming community. "Farmers are like a house with all the lights on but nobody's in" he would say. He was on thin ice in the bus depot, when he realised that two of the part-time drivers were farmers. They fitted in bus driving with lambing, sheep dipping and taking livestock to the market.

There were two drivers renowned for the speed they drove at; Fast Edwin for driving at breakneck speed and Turbo Toby for doing the opposite and driving vintage double decker buses very slowly. No one knew quite how The Elk acquired his nickname, though it may have emanated, years ago in the school playground.

The Yorkshireman was known for being blunt and consequently flashpoints with some passengers occurred on some rural routes. One such disagreement ended up in the 'Letters' page of the local paper with an indignant OAP moaning that he had to pay when he had a free pass.

"I'd have sued the sod if he'd put my name in the newspaper," he said through gritted teeth, "and what's more I didn't 'rudely snatch' his travel pass from his hands as he claims. I just told him he had to pay. I was just doing my job." The passengers soon learnt not to mess with the Yorkshireman – they would never win.

Rural routes can have their awkward moments. 99.9% of the time the passengers were charming and it was like a little club. They happily gossiped about what was going on in the local area. But woe betide, when a problem arose, it stuck out like a sore thumb. The relatively small population which inhabited the countryside meant that small spats became big problems in a short period of time. As a rural bus driver I found that I had to be a man for all parts. I was sometimes a counsellor, disciplinarian, advisor, peace-maker, director, tour guide, local historian and route finder. Passengers asked every kind of question. Bus drivers were in the thick of any dispute, as I found out to my peril, because a week after the Yorkshireman's run in with the whingeing passenger, a complaint arrived on the boss's desk against me. A passenger was saying that he had been short changed by 10p. He became obsessive about the matter and kept repeating that it was not the money that bothered him, but the principle. After the eighth fax which was sent in the early hours of the morning, suggesting that I should have stopped the bus with the passengers on and gone to the bank for some more change, the boss lost patience. He sent reams of legal jargon, essentially saying that if he sent any more faxes, it would be considered as harassment and he would look forward to meeting him in court. The faxes stopped.

This was on the route, which was known amongst the drivers as the 'Vallium Run'. It was eleven hours of driving and because you do not pick up many passengers, it could be extremely boring. All drivers had different ways of coping with the boredom.

The Vallium Run went through a market town which, since the bypass was completed had gained an increased reputation for its lawlessness and was viewed as a good place for a punch-up on a Friday or Saturday night. The town had recently been in the news when there was a full scale riot. The highlight of the day for drivers was to negotiate the anarchic parking which had become the norm in the town centre. It was a challenge to get past all the illegally parked cars in the High Street.

"Put yer foot down, lad," advised one of the elderly passengers. "Get on with yer, take no prisoners."

The sight of my bus in the middle of the road seemed to make angry motorists and boy racers even angrier. They tried their best to bully me off the road, driving straight at a nonexistent gap, shaking their fists, flashing their lights and hooting their horns.

"Go on son, you're bigger than they are. Keep going" my backseat driver would advise as we scraped by with millimetres to spare. The first time it happened it was disturbing, but, I soon got used to it and treated it like an average, everyday occurrence, as all the seasoned drivers at the company did.

Whereas the Vallium Run was unanimously viewed as turgid, the opposite could be said of the drivers who drove the sleeper buses which were hired out to the music industry for rock bands and their roadies to use on tours. One of the drivers was Howard. He once took one of the double-decker band buses on a tour around Amsterdam, a city notorious for its low bridges. Howard failed to notice this and the bus had numerous scrapes and dents as a result of connecting with the stonework. When he reported it to the company he began to receive texts from the boss addressed to JET, instead of the usual Howard. Phone messages saying JET do this, JET do that, JET go here, JET go there. When he asked why, he would never get an answer to his question. Finally, a few weeks later, a simple text appeared saying:

JET = Jug Eared Twat

and that it mainly referred to his adventures under the bridges, but was also a reference to his physical features as his ears did stick out a little.

The company had a second depot on the outskirts of Newcastle in an old pit village situated on top of a dank and windy hill, between a dual carriageway and the River Tyne. It had a Chinese Take-Away, which was so well known that some of the Newcastle United football players used to patronise it following training and there were some shops, turn of the century terraced houses and the bus garage. Being so small, it meant that the community was tightly knit and everybody knew about everybody else's business.

Some of the drivers used to live in the terraced houses next to the depot and only had a short walk to work.

I used to like visiting. It was a chance to catch up with some of the drivers who I rarely saw. They always had some new trick up their sleeves to teach me something new. A Glaswegian who sometimes worked for the company showed me how to get your own back at pedestrians. He had figured out if the windscreen washer tubes were set at the correct angle and if the the lever was pressed at the right time, a jet of soapy water would hit an unsuspecting passerby on the back of the neck. The victim would look up and down the street to see where the water had come from, looking everywhere except at the passing bus.

Fast Edwin, the fast driver, had a personalised number plate on his car which read 'Fast Edwin is 50', though no one knew whether that related to his age or the speed he drove at. He was a jovial fellow with a deep booming laugh who was much liked by the other drivers. He was an experienced bus driver and had even driven the non-striking miners to work in the Miners' Strike of 1984, at speed, with a police escort through aggressive picket lines and lines of policemen in front of the mine gates. Fast Edwin only had two speeds at which he drove ... fast and very fast. This brought about an above average number of complaints and certain organisations had requested that another driver be supplied.

Two passengers had nervously rang the boss to complain that

their driver had been speeding along a certain stretch of road.

"Not me" Fast Edwin had told them.

"Yes it was" said the passengers, "we knew for definite when you passed the flashing safety speed sign. It clearly said ... Your Speed is ... 52".

"Ah" said Fast Edwin.

"Ah" said the boss.

I was sent down to the Tyneside depot when things got busy. One thing I learnt quickly was the passionate and partisan support for one of the two major football teams in the North East. At first I naively said Newcastle United only to find the person was a Sunderland supporter and when I said Sunderland they would invariably be an avid follower of the Magpies.

So I thought up a way of being diplomatically evasive when the dreaded "Who do you support?" question was asked.

"Raith Rovers" I replied and was greeted always with stunned silence.

"Raith who? ... never heard of them...". It was the perfect result and I was never troubled again.

Two passengers once started trading jokes about their respective football teams across the aisle. "Why is Ruud Gullit (the then Newcastle United manager) speeding up the A69?" one of them asked me pointedly, obviously seeking to enlist my support against the other passenger.

"Dunno," I replied like a wet blanket, trying to avoid any sort of biased comment.

"It's the only way he can guarantee getting three points, of course!"

"Why you Macem bastard," said the other passenger, who was enraged by the insulting joke. "Ask the driver how you make a water feature in Sunderland?"

I started to feel uncomfortable. The already acidic atmosphere had the feeling that it was about to bubble over and that a fight could start. "Dunno," I repeated in a vain and feeble attempt of trying to diffuse the situation.

"Well, first you build a giant wall round the place, then you turn the taps on and fill it up."

That was the final straw. The two passengers stood up and faced off. Fisticuffs were imminent.

I thought enough was enough and stopped the bus. I got up from my seat and pretended to examine a lever above the exit door. Both men stopped talking about football and looked concerned at what I was doing.

"What's up, mate?" asked one.

"Is it broken?" asked the other.

"Yes," I replied furrowing my brow. "Yes, I am afraid so. Can I ask you to hold the lever while I waggle the switch. It is heavy, mind you and will take both of you."

They turned into obedient slaves and did exactly what I asked. As they stood by the door, arms raised and holding on to the lever tightly, I returned to the driver's seat. Almost in one movement, I pressed the button, opened the door, pushed the two men down the steps, out on to the pavement, pressed the button again, closed the door and drove off. The shocked men had recovered just enough from their tumble to punch the back of the bus and scream a few defamatory remarks as I drove away.

The bus returned unscathed to the yard with a few greasy knuckle prints to its rear panel. I parked it in the yard outside the bus depot. When descending the bus steps, I was always careful where I trod. At certain parts of the yard there were spots where drivers would drop the contents of their onboard toilets (this was before the days of strict regulation against polluting the environment). In addition to this unpleasantness, the local inhabitants would walk their dogs so there were invariably piles of dog shit everywhere. I usually trod on something organic. The rest of the yard had become a favourite place for fly tipping. There were piles of tarmac, bricks, oil, every metal part you could think of from a bus, bus seats, anything plastic and even the remains of a speed boat (minus its engine).

Living close by was an unofficial caretaker and her husband, who was a roofer and occasionally mended the depot's glass roof, which was often being shattered by well aimed bricks from the youths.

"How's your wife today?" I once asked him.

"She's fine but she keeps on taking those ugly pills."

They were an unusual couple. They were attached to their family but at the same time the husband was keen on having a good night out on the town. I occasionally went too and felt immediately that my education in drink related matters was widened. He introduced me to the best deals and the best drink which came from the supermarkets where lager could be bought for 60p a pint, the Italian fish and chip shop which sold under the counter Grappa, home distilled Rakia and Ouzo from his friends he used to visit abroad on his holidays and a local pub which sold a beer called Blackout, which was so strong, at around 15%, that the publican would only sell it in half pints and then only a maximum of two halves was permitted per customer.

"I've seen that many people passed out in the car park in wintertime because of two Blackouts, with their legs in the air, sticking out of some snowdrift, people might think I'm trying to give them hypothermia!" he proudly announced. The night I went, the temperature was too warm for snow, but there were still bodies upended in the flower beds, lying on flattened wallflowers.

'Keep-On-Taking-The-Ugly-Pills' used to be furious at his antics, when he passed out at the bar and had to be carried home. He came into the depot looking as if it had been a particularly heavy night. I marked his appearance down to drink, but I was wrong.

"I hit him when he's drunk 'til he's black and blue." she said.

They were very kind and took me into their house during my break, where they plied me full of coffee, when I waited to do the school run or return trip.

"You're better than that Cockney Ron," she said. "He barges his way in, says he quite fancies a bacon sarnie, drinks all my coffee, then falls asleep for three hours in my chair. I've learnt. Now when he knocks on the door I hide and pretend I'm not in."

Lunch used to be a tempestuous affair when the other drivers used to like to take me to a butcher's shop which doubled as a sandwich bar. It felt like it was a breeding ground for salmonella. "Lovely hot sandwiches" the drivers used to say. They were served by a grumpy, fat teenager, with excessively dyed blonde hair, who would growl at me when I entered the shop: "What do you want?" she would say in an irritated voice.

The counter was divided into two. The hot food was roasting and possibly irradiated by those powerful orange lights that keep food warm as all the meat was black in the middle and curled around the edges. It did not really matter because everything was smothered in thick, congealed brown gravy so that you forgot about the crinkly meat. Even the cold food was hot. It was cooked slowly by being in range of the warming lights and had a grey rather than the black appearance of the hot food.

That too came half smothered in gravy. When the lady served the hot food, drops of gravy would fly across the counter and splatter the cold hams, chickens and turkeys.

I used to time myself as to when the first rumblings in the bowels used to strike. It varied between 10 and 15 minutes, but sometimes I only managed 5 minutes. The other drivers seemed to have iron stomachs or perhaps they put a brave face on it. The depot would however often reverberate to the sound of breaking wind.

I learnt very quickly about the connection of being a bus driver and sensible eating. I learnt too that there is nothing worse than a flatulent bus driver, certainly in the eyes of the public. It was the a main cause for passengers to lose faith in their driver. If you had to make unplanned stops, then they started to actively detest you.

The belly rules the mind, as a Spanish friend often used to say. "Your belly rules all of our minds," an American passenger said to me the morning after the night before of excessive eating. Needless to say she did not leave a tip. I tend to eat Sushi these days. It is more lucrative.

CHAPTER 4

GOD, BUDDHISTS, MUSLIMS, JEWS, SCHOOLS, DRUNKS, SICKNESS and SEX

For some, life runs smoothly from day one. Everything falls into place, love, marriage, work. For others, like me, it was not so simple. If anyone had told me as a 24 year-old, when I worked in the horseracing world in the daytime and on sofas in dark corners of nightclubs that later in life I would become a bus driver, I wouldn't have believed them.

Unbeknown to me, I had a sneak preview of what life on the buses would be like on the first Wednesday in June in 1986 when I worked in the PR department of a bookie and was travelling to work on one of the biggest days of the year, Derby Day. 250,000 race goers and gypsies descended on Epsom Downs, causing traffic gridlock. Having left early however, I missed the worst of the traffic and only had to queue for the last few hundred yards before Tattenham Corner. The police had cordoned off all the approach roads and there was a one-way route into the course. I stopped directly behind an open-topped double-decker bus and an open-topped Mercedes Coupe.

The occupants of the Mercedes were an affluent and peaceful

looking couple on their way for a sociable day in the Members Enclosure. He was in a grey tailcoat and she in a Parisian designer silk dress and opulent wide brimmed straw hat and white gloves. It was a warm and bright June morning.

The party on the double-decker were dressed in black suits, sunglasses and bowler hats. They could have been in fancy dress, looking more like members of Madness or the Blues Brothers rather than racegoers. They were boisterous and looked as though they had been at the champagne since boarding the bus at dawn. Without warning, one of the party leant over the top and was promptly sick into the open top Mercedes. It was a direct hit on the straw hat and the morning coat received a large enough splattering to ruin the couple's day out. The woman froze and looked as if she had been caught in a snowstorm, she burst into tears. Her partner looked up at the top deck, snarled at the laughing passengers, leapt out of his car and boarded the bus.

The fight lasted only a few minutes before two passing constables broke it up. Within that time, he had downed four of the men. The woman had also boarded the bus and in between screaming obscenities, had put her weighty handbag to good use and had damaged a few others. There was a danger of someone being pushed over the edge of the top deck.

A dozen years later, I was standing in the aisle dealing with people being sick. Now it was sick schoolchildren, not drunk racegoers on my bus, on the twisty road through the Pennines which made it a challenge for even the sturdiest stomachs, so no wonder all the children were reaching for the sick bags. For more of a challenge there were motorbikes screaming round every corner. Around the sharpest corner on the route, a biker had appeared in the middle of the road, heading straight for the metal grill on the front of my bus. I glimpsed the rider's sheer terror through the visor of his helmet. He tensed up and must have thought that he was going to meet his maker, in an unglamorous way, courtesy of a bloody bus.

The bike wobbled wildly and swerved. I could only grip the steering wheel as I watched him in the mirror and waited for the impact. The crash came, but not as I expected. There was a gentle thud as he clipped the back end of the bus. It was enough for the rider and his machine to part company and I watched him roll over numerous times before lying prostrate along the broken white lines. I thought he was dead.

I rammed on the parking brake, jumped down and ran around the bend, fully expecting to see a body, but amazingly the biker was standing in the road, dusting himself down and using his hands to rock his helmeted head from side to side.

"No problem, mate," he smiled as he spoke in muffled tones and hastily mounted his bike and rode off into the sunset.

I returned to see how my retching schoolchildren were getting along.

* * * * *

I had no idea either that becoming a bus driver would bring me into contact with sex. I'd always thought it was an unglamorous industry with most un-sexy people who worked in it and therefore sex and buses made unlikely bedfellows. How wrong I was and I was soon to find out that the age-old jokes about cars with steamy windows or rocking caravans, which stereotypically gave the impression that there was naughty business going on equally applied to buses. The first time I viewed a parked bus rocking from side to side, I thought it was because some of the passengers were having a fight. But it was something completely different and I soon learnt that if I saw a rocking bus in a lay-by to drive on to the next one and not stop to investigate.

I was once sitting in the coach park beside a castle in a city centre, when the local service bus from Scotland parked next to me, keeping its engine running. I looked over at the empty driver's seat and assumed that the driver must have got off the bus for a stretch, a pee or a fag break. But he was nowhere to be seen. I looked down the back and thought I saw something white moving on the back seat. Initially, I thought he must be reading a newspaper. He wasn't. When I looked closer, what I actually saw was a pair of large white buttocks going up and down with two white legs pointing straight up towards the roof of the bus.

I was struck with a queasy embarrassment and looked quickly in the other direction at the passing trains. After a few minutes I heard a knock on my window. It was the driver. He was straightening his tie. His girlfriend was standing close behind smoothing the wrinkles in her blouse and skirt. She seemed to be wearing the same uniform as the man and could well have worked for the same company.

"Mum's the word, mate," he said, staring at me and raising an index finger to his lips. His girlfriend blushed and giggled nervously.

"Do you do this regularly?" I asked him. The words slipped out without any thought and I fully expected a punch in the nose.

He stiffened then laughed. "Yeah, when I can, mate. You have to be quick, mind, as I only have five minutes before I have to get back on service" He looked over at the girlfriend who was still blushing and giggling and continued, "but we manage don't we Kelly."

On the other hand, I saw the very opposite kind of behaviour from the cleanest and politest members of our society. The Buddhists from a local monastery never did anything contrarian or unkind and never had a nasty word to say about anybody. Sex seemed to be a million miles from their thoughts.

"Good Morning," I'd say to them as they boarded the bus.

"Well, thank you. Thank you very much," they would each reply.

It took me by surprise. Driving buses had made me cynical and my initial reaction was that they were taking the mickey. But they weren't. They all said exactly the same thing with the same genuine enthusiasm. In fact, they said something positive to almost anything I uttered. It was the most charming tour I had ever taken and the time flew by.

It was too good to last and I came down to earth with a bump when I returned to the depot and saw the boss.

"What a gloriously beautiful day," I said to the boss in a carefree way, I thought the Buddhists would have been proud of me.

"Is there something wrong with you?" he replied, looking thoroughly disturbed. "Tool" he muttered as he wandered back into the office.

He was right. It was only a couple of days before I fulfilled his prophecy and proved that I was a tool when I took a group of Methodists to Robin Hood's Bay. The bus I took had a time saving quirk. It was possible to fill up the bus's diesel tank by removing the keys from the ignition, whilst keeping the engine running and using the other key on the fob to open the diesel tank cover. Any sensible bus driver would immediately replace the keys in the ignition after fuelling up and before setting off on the journey.

I didn't. In my hurry I forgot.

I left the keys on top of the diesel pump, locked the depot up and drove off to the church where I was due to pick up the Methodists. It was not for well over an hour that I realised what had happened and by that time we were well on the way to the coast.

What was I going to do?

It was a hot day and because I had no key, I couldn't turn off the engine. There was a chance that the bus would run out of fuel, or overheat as it was a steaming hot day. As a last resort I rang the office to see what they suggested.

'Idiot, fool, tool,' said the boss.

I didn't tell the Methodists, they were in high spirits and this would only have spoilt their day. They were different from many Methodist groups I had taken in the past, who had been dour and preached the benefits of temperance and abstinence. The first thing they said, when we arrived at our destination, was, "Where's the pub?"

An unlikely solution was found. The boss managed to find a bus company in York, about 50 miles away, which had the same make and model of bus that I was driving and, what's more, it had a spare key. I sneaked off to York when I heard singing coming from the pub. The Methodists would be occupied for some time. I arrived back in Robin Hood's Bay two hours later and the group was still singing and none the wiser that there had been a problem.

I always enjoyed driving in June and July. Everyone was always in holiday mood and the atmosphere was good on the buses. The best summer seaside trip I did involved taking a Working Men's Club from Gateshead, which was then one of the last big clubs in the North East. It had over 4000 members and once a year they hired six buses to go for a day out to Seahouses on the north Northumberland coast, taking over 300 men.

They were very good natured, honourable and determined to enjoy their trip from the outset. Soon after 8am they were tucking into their first pint of bitter of the day in the club. They maintained strict club rules and did not permit their members to eat or drink on the buses. Instead the lockers of the buses were loaded with cans of beer and cheese savoury, corned beef or ham and pease pudding stotties.

It was a tradition that forty-five minutes up the road the six buses would pull into a lay-by and all 300 club members disembarked. The sandwiches and the beer were unloaded and they milled around on the verge. I was sitting in the driver's seat of my bus when I looked out the door to see an old man standing there. He was using his left hand to hold the beer can, from which he was drinking. At the same time, he was using his right hand to hold his 'old man' and was peeing like a dog on the front wheel of the bus.

He turned, saw my dropped jaw and said: "Dinna worry, mate. One in. One oot."

We went on to Seahouses where it was hard to see anything as there was a sea fret. This in no way inhibited their enjoyment as they headed straight for the pubs and the bookies who were only open because they had forgotten that this club was coming. They had closed for the day the year before; the club members had been told that the turf accountant had been tipped off about the club's outing and had taken the day off, remembering the hammering he had taken from the punters the previous year, nearly being cleaned out.

For lunch they tended to congregate in Seahouses' numerous fish and chip shops. Each chippy had advertising boards outside the door, proudly proclaiming, 'Fish Locally Caught'. A local bus driver disputed this fact,

"They're being economical with the truth,' she said. 'Yes it is caught locally ... but it is caught by the Norwegian fishing fleet, taken back to Oslo, gutted, filleted and sent back frozen."

No one seemed to care and it did not deter sales as all the bus drivers and myself piled into the nearest shop.

In the evening all 300 men went to a hotel for a sit down dinner. The six bus drivers were invited too.

"You can't be without your bait, man. We like to look after you bus drivers," said one of the organisers. It was traditional, wholesome North Eastern fare.

The beef was well done, so well done that it was crispy. This was hidden by a giant Yorkshire pudding which had been placed on top with thick brown gravy cascading over the edge. Another waitress appeared shortly after the plate had been put down and said, "Would you like any more gravy love?" Most said yes and their plates were turned into culinary swimming pools. The huge jug of gravy was soon empty.

I wasn't hungry. My plate was snatched away by a fellow driver. Other drivers could not finish their plates and Mervyn scraped the leftovers on to his plate and finished them, before moving on to the sherry trifle or apple pie, swamped in custard. He managed to eat another five plates. This was not an isolated incident as he was once asked to leave an eat-as-much-as-you-like Chinese buffet. No one had ever been asked to leave before, but the proprietor had had enough, when his chefs couldn't cook enough to keep Melvyn contented, profits were being halved and there was no food for the other customers.

The variety of life as a bus driver meant that the next day was another long day of a different kind. It was spent with the Bangladeshi community, who had ordered two buses to take people to a wedding near Wakefield. The bride's family were in one bus and the bridegroom's family in the other. They were generous and polite, but hopeless when it came to punctuality or knowing where they were going. I was to learn that Bangladeshi weddings went on for a long period of time.

"It can go on for two weeks," said one of the family.

The other bus driver nearly fainted. "But I told my wife I would be back in time for dinner"

"You will be back, tonight," the organiser said directly, "but late …
v-e-r-r-y late." The bus company had done its usual trick of un-
derplaying the length of the job. "It won't be after 6 or 7," the boss
had said disingenuously.

The family and wedding guests were smartly dressed. The bride
and bridegroom were colourful and beautiful. The day started by
going round to the front door of many houses and waiting for
twenty minutes while the families talked and argued about the
time they were going to leave.

They were insistent that we arrived on time as they would be
leaving no later than 8am. We left at 11.30am. The journey was un-
problematic until we were within three miles of the venue. Then it
took a further hour to find the pub.

The actual wedding was more like a piece of theatre. In the middle
of the room, in a shimmering satin tent, the bride sat on a pile of
silk covered cushions. There were people applying turmeric paste
and henna to the bride. The guests seemed to give the couple en-
velopes filled with cash.

They asked the drivers to join the party and we sat next to a cocky
stretch limo driver who had also been hired for the day. He
delightedly got his comeuppance as he was always showing off
about how knowledgeable he was about curry.

"I like my Chicken Madras hot" he proudly announced at our table.

"Well that is Indian food," corrected one of the guests. "This is a
Bangladeshi wedding."

"Oh yeah, of course," the limo driver went on, pretending to be an
expert. "I'm looking forward to the King Prawn Vindaloo, then."

"No, no, no," said the guest, "that is also from India, but of

Portuguese origin and ..." The driver's face went the colour of as ripe tomato and he began to stand up. He was so angry, I thought he was about to strike the wedding guest, when the food arrived at the table. It was some sort of chicken curry, served by waiters from plastic washing buckets. There followed a succession of waiters holding more washing up buckets with different curries. The smell of the spices was fantastic, and the food was delicious but, boy was it hot; it was super hot. The limo driver with his peroxide blonde hair lasted two mouthfuls before he ran out the room, shouting, "I'm on fire! I'm on fire! Help me." The wedding guests clapped and we never saw him again.

The rest of the day was spent driving the bus up every cul-de-sac and narrow one way street in Leeds. After the wedding feast there followed this muddling conversation:

"We want to see our cousin – can you take us to him?" asked the organiser.

"Where does he live?" asked my fellow bus driver.

"Leeds."

"Where exactly in Leeds?"

"Leeds 11. We think."

"That is a big chunk of Leeds. Can you be more specific? Which street? Do you know the address?"

"I do not know, but I will know when I get there," said the optimistic organiser. And so reluctantly we went on a wild goose chase around Leeds.

"I am thinking we are nearly there. Yes Yes. I am thinking this is the street. Maybe. Yes, Yes ... oh no, maybe definitely not." After the thirteenth time of the organiser getting off the bus and knocking on someone's door, being told his cousin did not live there and being politely requested to remove himself and his bus from their street, that was the time his determination waned and he decided to call it a day.

We got back to the depot with three minutes left of our permitted fifteen hour shift.

From the sublime to the ridiculous, I used to take parties nightclubbing all night at a hotel near Teesside. It was the most famous club in the North and attracted visitors from as far away as Birmingham, Manchester and Leicester as well as the North East and Borders. Being so large and hosting more than 3000 hot and sweaty clubbers, it was more like a cattle market.

The coach park was full of rust buckets. No company in their right mind would send any new or nice bus on a job such as this, because the clubbers turned into animals. By first light, on the return journey, they would have thrown up, slashed the seats, sprayed paint on to the ceiling or scratched graffiti into the bus windows. The bus companies tolerated this behaviour as long as the damage was not too great. The money was good. Even though the wages were more than reasonable, no bus drivers ever wanted to do this job and a lot of arm twisting by the boss went on behind the scenes.

The drivers would take their sleeping bags and lie on the back seat in the hope of having a couple of hours sleep. This rarely happened. The early night would be taken up with most of the drivers standing in clusters, ogling at the arriving bus loads of merry mooning girls who would drive past. They were not yet drunk enough and still in control of most of their bodily functions. The later it got, the more aggressive and plastered the clubbers became and that was when the fights started.

I took a party from my local village. Their behaviour that night was not violent, but shaming enough for some of them to still look embarrassed when they see me now. It is bad luck for them that I can remember how each and every one of them behaved.

The bus rolled into the coach park at around 10pm and we left at 6am. I filled twenty bin bags with empty bottles and took them out of the bus, on the journey down and twelve on the return, bulging with empty alcopop bottles and cigarette butts. There were three enforced 'pee' stops on the way down and three 'puke' stops on the return. Most fell into a coma just as the sun rose, after a full fried breakfast at a service station.

One of the group's legs gave way and he sat on the rear seat, repeating over and over again, "I want to go to the toilet, and I know that it is so far to go, that when I get there I won't want to go."

Stag weekends are also perilous events for bus drivers. A colleague once took a family on a stag weekend to Hull. They turned out to be a busload of hoods and gangsters. Some were out on probation. The trip proved to be a disastrous weekend as four of the party were arrested for possession of cocaine.

"I was very naive," said the driver, "because when they said to me, do you fancy a line? I innocently thought that they were being friendly and wanted me to chip in some cash for their Lottery syndicate."

He told the story where all bus drivers stories are usually told, in the middle of a coach park surrounded by a group of drivers. One of the others turned and said, "You won't bloody believe what's happened in my village," said the driver. His facial muscles became animated and he started to twitch, as he went on, "The ducks have been removed from our village pond because the young incomer mothers complained about over-active sexual activities of the drakes, which they said was frightening their children."

The driver on the other side was unhappy with and complained about everything. He talked in serious tones, had no sense of humour, but managed to be amusing without realising it. He had just parked his ageing double-decker and was moaning about a group who had been on his bus the day before. One of the passengers was truly awful and reduced the hostess to tears with his insults and general callousness.

"I was furious and I thought I'll f***ing fix him. And I did," he said in an intense and bitter way, though the hint of a smile was beginning to take shape. "I swopped with the hostess and served the drinks. I gave him a cup of tea. But after a minute and then at varying intervals he kept coming down to the other driver and complaining that there was something in his tea and that it did not taste very nice at all."

He stopped as he could barely control himself anymore, before continuing. "Yes he kept moaning that something was floating on the surface." Well, the other driver examined the cup, put his fingers into the tea, felt around a bit and retrieved a pair of false teeth. "Oh good," he said, "I've been looking for them everywhere," and put them back into his mouth.

He slapped his thighs with contentment at having got one over on a passenger. "You should have seen rude boy," he continued, "he turned a funny colour, went back to his seat and we never heard another squeak out of him for the rest of the journey."

* * * * *

A staple diet of most companies was the transportation of ramblers, in a mixture of fluorescent coloured clothing, an odd assortment of floppy hats, rucksacks with aromas of stale cheese savoury sandwiches and a pairs of ski poles. The majority were over 70 and many were short haired, bespectacled, feisty, politically left of centre, Guardian reading, Greenpeace supporting ladies who strode out purposefully. These liberal women were accompanied by a minority of mouse-like menfolk, who lagged behind and were quite possibly thinking of the next pint they are going to be allowed to have.

These groups, because of their age and activity were known by some drivers as "the walking dead". But they gave an enormous chunk of business to the bus companies, regardless of their demanding and forthright ways and were a regular feature on most weekends between April and November. It was rare that they cancelled and only then in exceptionally adverse weather conditions.

The first time I took them I asked them how long they had been rambling for.

"We're not ramblers," they would point out with great indignation. "We are a Walking Club, established long before the Ramblers. We've been around for over a century."

Some drivers could not bear them. Polluting Pete was one who detested them. Once in the pouring rain a group of people looking like drowned rats, asked if they could get back on the bus.

"Certainly not," he replied. "European Law clearly states that a driver's rest period must be in complete peace, without any interruptions from anyone. Anyway, you are ramblers and ramblers are supposed to WALK!" They trudged off miserably, but it became an uneasy relationship between them and the driver for evermore.

Even Bert, the other regular driver who was patient and usually had a most genial nature lost patience with them and one day put his foot down over the switchback road near Rothbury. When they got home one lady who looked more rattled than the others went up to him and said, "I've been travelling on buses for 75 years and this is the first time I've been upended out of my seat."

Each year this century-old Walking Club went for an annual week's walking holiday to an hotel on the Yorkshire coast, between Scarborough and Whitby. The hotel was started by members of the Rowntree family, owners of the York chocolate factory. In the 1920s they had the vision of opening up a conference/holiday centre for those who worked in education, social service or other voluntary and charitable organisations. Like many of the chocolate-making families around the world the Rowntrees were Quakers and great philanthropists, similar to Hersheys in the USA and Cadbury's at Bourneville in the West Midlands. They were keen to encourage adult education and the original vision of the founders has changed little over the years.

The old part of the hotel still contained many reminders of John Rowntree with framed pictures of every chocolate wrapper produced by Rowntrees and Rowntree Mackintosh. The catering revolved around wholesome food, and the ramblers wolfed it down.

The serving staff met their match with some of the more feisty members of the club. Breakfast started with a complaint from one upset rambler who lambasted the young boy waiter for producing underdone toast.

"Its bread," replied the boy.

"Oh," said the rambler, momentarily taken aback. "Well, take it back anyway and bring me proper toast."

Things did not improve at dinner. Even a long day's hard walking didn't seem to diminish their energy or ability to complain when something was not to their liking.

"The lamb chops are too overdone," pointed out one lady to the waitress. "It causes us problems with our false teeth."

But the more the week went on, the more you got to know and

admire them. Yes they were pernickety; "What's that bag for?" I stupidly asked, thinking we were short of room on the bus. "It's for my slippers, of course. I take them everywhere," said the owner.

As their driver I spent a lot of time with them and soon got used to their spirited and opinionated ways. They were an easy and well mannered group to take, once you were used to their straight talking. They would take their bus driver under their wing. Naturally they demanded a lot. They would want the bus to go up some devilishly narrow Yorkshire lanes and the waiting around times would be long. But they used to feed the driver sweets and titbits and packed lunches, invariably meaning that I would return home a kilo or two heavier.

For octogenarians and nonagenarians, they were incredibly fit and sprightly. They would step out and easily out-walk far younger groups. The night times were packed full of entertainment, from whist drives to quiz nights to dominoes to dancing the Mississippi Dip. The next morning after one particular dance evening, it was worrying to be accosted by one female octogenarian.

"Hello lover," she said, fluttering her eyelashes. I ran for cover under the bus, and lay on my back pretending to look for an oil leak, until she lost interest and went off for breakfast. From then on I made sure the ladies were always in pairs.

A special couple called Gerald and Hyacinth, celebrated their Golden Wedding Anniversary. Hyacinth, without doubt, wore the trousers. She was immaculately turned out, always in smart clothes and never a hair out of place. Gerald was charming and quietly played second fiddle, never ruffling any feathers and was equally well dressed in a tweed jacket with leather patches under the elbows. One cause of his lack of verve was revealed when Gerald told of his engagement and of how his confidence was dented when he went to ask Hyacinth's mother for her daughter's hand in marriage.

"Well, I suppose it's better than nothing," the mother had said to Gerald.

They had a very spoilt and over pampered dog called Gonzo. Gonzo was a Shitsu and was overly sweet. The strictest rules were adhered to and he was never allowed off a lead. Hyacinth and Gonzo would sit in the front seat of the bus. He was always propped on the finest cushion. On one trip a hairnet fell off the seat and wrapped itself around the gear lever.

"This must be Hyacinth's," I said handing it back to Gerald.

"Oh no," he replied, "it's Gonzo's. He never eats his dinners without wearing it. It stops his ears falling into the food."

* * * * *

Sporting trips were of a very mixed bag. Tottenham Hotspur FC had a supporters club based in the North West. They would hire the bus at a very good rate and two drivers would take them down to White Hart Lane in North London. They would watch the match and immediately after the final whistle, they turned tail and headed back North. There was just time for a kebab from one of the numerous Turkish restaurants in Tottenham, which had a large Turkish community. It was one of the parts of the job I relished, the ability to try foods from all round the world, owing to the diverse range of take-aways and restaurants I would invariably find my bus parked next to.

When we arrived following a six or seven hour drive, a Belgian bus was invariably already parked up. It was depressing to think that it was faster to get to Tottenham from Charleroi than it was from North West England. The return journey was worse as it got dark soon after we left. The fans started chanting as soon as they returned to the bus and the drivers had to suffer countless renditions of "it's 2-1, we beat the scum". They were the meanest lot of passengers I have ever taken. They demanded all sorts of special treatment such as extra drop-off points and we tried our best for them. When we arrived back at the starting point, well after midnight, they repaid us by leaving the bus in a filthy state and not giving any kind of tip.

They stopped using our bus company and the drivers heaved a sigh of relief. Another company had slightly undercut us. Good riddance we all thought.

* * * * *

I found myself regularly driving a rugby club around the country for their weekend matches. This club was identical to others in that their post-match behaviour was consistent and out of control. The days were equally long, if not longer than the visits to the London football grounds. The blowing of the final whistle was a signal to hit the bar and start drinking. All team members were required to then keep drinking until they couldn't stand up anymore. The return journeys became nightmarish.

The day always began like a military operation. The organiser had allotted pick-up points and times which he liked to stick to. He would sit in the bus, looking at his watch and making sure that the pick-up times were punctual. If anything went wrong there would be a stern look and a grumpy response which culminated in a sharp outburst.

"Bloody hell," he would yell and slam his hand down on his clipboard.

But generally they weren't so bad and the players were a genial bunch when they were sober. Every week they would play a different team in the league. The away games would take them to places such as Dudley, Macclesfield, Cambridge, Bedford and even Southend. There was a regular driver who had been driving them for years and knew their habits. I only always came along when a double driver was needed, which was quite often because they always insisted on stopping somewhere for a night out after the match.

It was after a game against a Midlands team that things took a turn for the worse. After several hours in the bar with the opposing team, they boarded the bus and began to drink in earnest in training for their big night out. They were champion drinkers. Some of them were better drinkers than rugby players. Only nine of them boarded the bus and between Spaghetti Junction and Penrith, a journey of no more than 2½ hours, they downed 187 large cans of bitter and lager. The beer that they didn't drink was sprayed on the aisle floor, in preparation for a game of human skittles. This involved lubricating the floor until it was like a river, then throwing a person stomach downwards, as hard as they could from the back to the front of the bus. The winner was the one whose head hit the gear stick the most times.

187 cans were an even more impressive total, when you consider that two of the players were Methodists from an island in the South Pacific who did not drink at all. They sat with headphones on at the front of the bus, gently humming to themselves and ignoring the riotous games going on behind them, as they listened to Polynesian Methodist hymns.

On another return trip from Macclesfield, a player was sick into the on-board lavatory. "Leave it to us," said the others, "we'll sort it." I thought no more about it and assumed they would simply clean up the mess and mop the floor. But they had other ideas. It happened to be a lovely evening as we drove over Shap summit. It was therefore surprising to suddenly see cars passing the bus with their wipers going when it was not raining. The occupants seemed to stare across at me and I thought that they didn't look over pleased. Looking more closely at the passing cars, the wipers seemed to be clearing away a blue liquid. Some of the windscreens had brown lumps on them and what appeared to be balls of white paper.

Then it clicked.

Blue liquid? Brown lumps? White paper? Oh my God, I thought, that could only mean one thing. The cretins had pulled the handle underneath the lavatory, which drops the chemical toilet, emptying all its contents.

The onboard bus lavatory has to be filled with a mixture of a potent blue chemical liquid and water, before it can be used. When it was full, a drain had to be found. The bus was then parked over the drain and the pipe was aligned with the grate before the handle could be pulled and the waste could only then be emptied. If the handle was pulled while the bus was in motion, something completely different happened. The contents were sprayed across a large area, in a similar manner to how a gritter distributed salt and grit on to roads in winter. So the overtaking cars in the middle and fast lanes of the M6 were being covered. I could imagine the car owners having to visit the car wash the next day.

It would have been nice to have said that this was a one-off misdemeanour. It wasn't. The people of Yorkshire, on the other side of the Pennines suffered the same fate on a return trip from Hull. The rugby club had chosen the quiet market town of Knaresborough for their night out. The police were nervous when they saw them arrive but were most patient and for some time adopted a live and let live attitude. They shadowed the team as they got drunker and louder, and tried to gently usher them back on to the bus. The straw that broke the camel's back was the antics of the Club Secretary, who in full view of the police, waddled up to the corporation's new raised flower bed in the bus station, swaying from side to side. He unzipped his flies and proceeded to pee over the pelargoniums. A watching Police Sergeant's eyes narrowed before he exploded with rage and frogmarched the organiser back on to the bus.

"Get them out of here. And get them out of here NOW!" shouted the Sergeant. As if he had not made the point, he sent a squad car to follow us up the motorway until we were 20 miles away from Knaresborough.

Shortly after these trips, the Secretary announced, "If anyone spews, it's a £50 club fine plus they have their noses rubbed in it and be hit by the driver."

"That's a bit of pot calling the kettle black," an anonymous voice piped up from somewhere down the back.

Occasionally I would be lucky enough to go to a sporting event which was legendary and was talked about for many years later, even if it meant that I never left the coach park or actually saw the magical event. The Pieman and I went to one of these when we transported 55 Sunderland supporters to Wembley Stadium for the Division One Play- Off Finals. Sunderland were playing Charlton Athletic and we listened to an exhilarating match on the bus radio, with the door of the bus open so that we could hear the roars and cheers emanating out of the roof of the massive stadium. The noise often drowned the radio commentary as more and more goals were scored. At 4-4 even the commentators seemed to need a change of clothing and their commentary became incomprehensible as their voices deteriorated into a throaty hoarseness of ecstasy.

In the middle of this great excitement a surreal sight presented itself as a group walked into the Coach Park, men in glasses and highly coloured Goretex jackets armed with notebooks, pencils, cameras and video cameras – the bus spotters. They were the poor relations of the train spotters, as bus drivers liked to describe them and were constantly made fun of. They must have been very resilient as they seemed to spend most of their time in windy and wet bus stations and coach parks. Wembley was a magnet for all types of buses. Because the customers were football fans, whose reputation preceded them, most bus companies would send their oldest buses, in case of hooliganism and vandalism. But everything had an upside and this was therefore a bus spotter's paradise.

The old Volvo, the Pieman and I were driving, seemed to be drawing a great deal of attention and these silent multi-coloured figures swarmed around us, frantically filling in their notebooks and taking pictures. They were in a world of their own and oblivious to the great sporting event going on in the stadium. Sunderland were beaten on penalties and the fans rolled back on to the bus in despondent mood. The drive back North is always a long affair. This May evening the atmosphere was funereal. Silence reigned and the families sat in their grief, staring out the window, before nodding off by the time we passed the Watford Gap. Hardly a word was uttered the whole trip.

Apart from football and rugby tours, I would be asked to drive occasional one-offs such as a Scottish Ladies Bowls Club who were going to play a tournament in Great Yarmouth. They were a wow. Before the ladies got on to the bus, there were signs that this was not going to be a quiet trip. One of the husbands came up to me and shook me warmly by the hand and said meaningfully: "Thank God you are taking her. Now I can have a peaceful holiday for a week. Can you please take her for two?"

They all had heavy bags which should have held their bowling equipment.

"You must have a lot of extra kit in your bags," I said as I puffed and panted and struggled to put their heavy luggage in the boot.

"Like hell we do," replied a worried looking lady. "That's our whisky bottles. You just be careful with them."

The bottles clinked against the hard bowling balls which were embedded in their suitcases. One lady had even gone so far as to hollow out the inside of a ball and fill it with whisky or barley juice as she called it.

"Aye, I usually take it abroad, on holiday with me. I find it's more than handy when bringing back in the duty free."

"Right now," said one of the husbands, rather too loudly before the bus left, "I'm off to the bar now, for a pint of heavy without fear of being henpecked."

The bus left at 7.45am. By 8 o'clock, the whisky was flowing freely. By 9 o'clock they were well away and as we hit the motorway, wild things were happening in the back seat, as cars and vans were passing, flashing their lights and blowing their horns. They had been holding up a placard which read, "Honk if you want it." At Penrith I handed them over to another driver who conducted the tour. The Irvine ladies gave me a warm send off with a word of caution and advice that I should always adhere to: "Be like us and don't drink too little, dear. And remember. Whisky is fine, but too much water makes you rust. Cheerio."

When I later saw the driver he said that it had continued in the same vein for the whole week in Great Yarmouth and that they had introduced him into their philosophy of waterless whisky. He complained that he suffered with the painful after-effects.

* * * * *

There were downright nasty days such as taking the Girl Guides to a County Durham estate. A more correct description would have been a muddy lane, during a tropical style rainstorm, on some far outpost of the estate where the Scouts and Girl Guides had struck their camps. Everything went wrong which could have gone wrong and we were all covered in mud from head to foot. The bus interior looked like the aftermath of a gunge attack, the equipment was extremely heavy and needed to be pulled a quarter of a mile up the lane, everyone was cold, wet and extremely irritable. All the windows in the bus steamed up and the heating did not work, but that seemed to be rock bottom and it was as if nothing else could go wrong.

But, naturally it did.

There was a notoriously bad right hand bend as you entered the picturesque little town of Staindrop. Fortunately the bus was going slowly when for some reason the extreme rivers of water on the road obviously became too much for her and she decided to go straight on rather than follow the right hand corner. Directly ahead there were some terraced houses. In one of the front windows there were two elderly faces which had turned away from the television and were staring out the window with increasing concern. The bus hit the curb with some force, but miraculously it bounced it around the road back on to its correct course. The Girl Guides were so exhausted that they did not notice what was going on.

Months later, I would always think of the old couple staring out of the window with horrified looks, thinking that a bus might shortly be arriving in their living room. I did see a For Sale sign outside the front door, when I drove past a year later and figured they must have thought that enough was enough.

It was no surprise, then, that the next day I was discussing what to do in the event of the death of a passenger on your bus, when you were deep in the south of France with a driver who had just returned from this surreal experience. It happened on a coach tour when the bus was heading home along the autoroute. A very old man unbuckled his seat belt and headed for the onboard toilet. He seemed to spend a very long time in the cramped cubicle. At the next service station one of the passengers decided to check and found him dead, possibly having had a heart attack. Because of the small space in the toilet, he was still leaning up at a 45 degree angle.

This was a nightmare scenario for the two drivers. They were sad that they had lost one of their passengers, but there was the far more worrying thought that French and European Regulations were so horrendous and fraught with bureaucratic claptrap, that it would mean long delays, much form filling and questioning by the Gendarmerie. So they took the decision to leave the body in exactly the same place in the onboard lavvy, making him appear more dignified as they pulled up the zip on his trousers.

It was still a grotesque sight. The dead old man, frozen as if in a sculpture paying homage to his last activity, similar to the Mannequin Pis in Brussels. The door was locked and the drivers drove hell for leather to Calais, holding their breath as they went through French Customs, on to the boat and finally arriving in Dover. They needn't have worried because the French customs officers were on a tea break and the docks were deserted.

The English customs officers were the opposite of their French compatriots. They were alert and eagle eyed. They had a knack and a nose for sniffing out problems at a distance. The drivers tried to pre-empt their suspicions by telling them that they did not count the passengers on to the boat in Calais and only when they counted them on in Dover did they discover the dead body. So he must have died whilst on the ferry.

"I don't think so," said the suspicious officer.

"No, no it's true," wailed the drivers.

"It's not true because I've never seen a recently deceased body in quite such an advanced state of rigor mortis," said the customs lady with mounting anger in her voice. "He's as stiff as a board. Now get yourselves and your passengers out of here and don't bother us again."

The drivers couldn't believe their luck. The customs officers had shown them some leniency. She had understood and seemed to empathise with a tricky situation. On reflection they might have had the same thought. The same horrendous thought of the pile of paperwork which would land on their desks and the potential for a protracted investigation and awkward legal situation might have been too awful to contemplate. The next police station outside the port inherited the problem.

The mere thought of having to cope with a dead body on my bus is always something which sends shivers down my gullet. I don't know what I would do or how I would react. Thus far I have not had to face up to this problem – but never say never.

Perhaps the biggest part of the job of being a bus driver was the school related business. Almost daily there were school trips to a variety of museums, visitor centres and places to do with dinosaurs, Romans, Egyptians or Victorians. Because of the state of school budgets and the increase in the cost of hiring a bus, school trips were in danger of being scaled back or even disappearing altogether. Hence trips in the North East tended to be to places that offered value for money and were often free or cheap and not too far away.

In line with the rest of the country, there was also a problem with a percentage of unfit, spoilt, over-mothered children. I ran into some when I took a school to a museum to Newcastle. There was a walk from the bus to the museum, it began to drizzle. The children started to whine. "There, there," said the parents. The teachers raised their eyes to heaven. After 100 yards, they cried. Their feet ached and they were not going to go another step. "There, there," said the parent helpers. The teachers raised their eyes skywards again and headed back to the bus. They sat on the bus eating their packed lunches. The children were distraught. The parents were clucking around them like over-protective hens, giving foot massages in some cases. The teachers sat at the front chomping on their sandwiches and raised their eyes upwards, not to heaven, but to the clock on the bus, in the vain hope that it was time to return to school.

The teachers were mainly practical and matter of fact. The good ones were quiet and you could see that the children adored them. The less good were the ones who shouted at the children. Though teachers in general possessed clear articulate speech and I once mistakenly asked a Gateshead teacher if she would like to use the bus's microphone. She looked appalled and said: "Thank you, no. I don't need a microphone. I'm a TEACHER!"

I had never taken much notice of the fact that most teachers have loud voices and certainly did not need any electrical gadget to increase their volume. It only hit home when I took a group of Dutch schoolchildren back to Manchester for their flight home and I asked the Dutch teachers, who had spent a week visiting schools in the Carlisle area what they thought of British schools. They were shocked at how many teachers shouted at their students which would never be allowed to happen in Holland.

One of the major problems on any school bus was travel sickness. Teachers tried every way to distract the pupils. "Play I-Spy" or "look out of the window – look at the lovely clouds" they would say before finally resorting to fear tactics , "Johnnie, don't even think about it – it'll be detention if you do," said one teacher.

Most teachers sat at the front of the bus and ignored what was going on behind them. Some were kind and consolatory, some were cheery and tried to make a joke of it all, "Pass the Happy Bucket," one cheerfully described the ubiquitous sick bucket which was a mandatory accessory on any school trip.

"Tuck your trousers into your socks, lad" said one of the more direct headteachers after one of his boys had had a terrible stomach upset.

"Don't worry son," said another teacher, "you are going to be on the stage one day."

"Aye, scrubbing it," said the boy sitting next to him who was holding his nose and retching at the same time.

It was one of the parts of the job I detested. After a very sick journey, the thought of having to return back to the depot and clean the bus was unappealing. When teachers made brash remarks, I often wanted to say something, but tact was always the better part of valour and my intervention would only have worsened the atmosphere.

The bus company I worked for transported many schools overcoming the problems of operating in the North Pennines where the roads were windswept, bumpy with steep gradients and tight bends. Any school coming from the West Midlands or Lancashire to the outward bound centre had an awkward journey. To get there the bus on leaving the M6 at Penrith, was faced a switchback journey, climbing and descending rapidly to Alston. No child or teacher relished the prospect of facing the much talked about route 122 corners to take in twenty minutes. The only way for a sick free journey was to put a DVD on, blast cold air through the bus and drive very, very slowly. The slower drivers seemed to be luckier, the speed merchants seemed to average between three and eight sick children per journey.

The noise was awful and the smell was even worse. It sometimes took months for the stink to come out of the seats. No amount of cleaners, detergents or disinfectants made much difference. It always depended on what they ate and how the teachers looked after them. Good schools gave the children water only and forbade any form of eating. Bad schools allowed them to eat anything. Some actively encouraged devouring as many different varieties of crisps or chewy sweets they could. The evidence of empty crisp packets and sweet papers was left strewn across the floor of the bus. Half eaten chewy sweets landed on the heater grills, liquefied and solidified in a sticky and immoveable mass on the floor. The used chewing gum had been stuck under the seat.

By far the worst were schools from the North. I had a sense of dread when children boarded the bus reeking of fried food, which meant they had earlier munched through a hearty breakfast likely to have consisted of large slices of black pudding sitting on top of fried egg, sausage, bacon, beans and fried bread, with the addition of fried tomatoes or mushrooms as a healthy afterthought. The 122 bends were waiting for them.

My life was about to change forever, and would mean that I would have to stop driving for the bus company at the top of the hill. At the age of 38, I was finally getting married. This was much to the joy and amazement of my mother who had given up any hope of grandchildren as neither myself or my brother had looked like finding a suitable partner, let alone producing offspring. I was going to move to my wife's house on the seaside, which meant having to find another job. One of the last jobs I was asked to do, was to take a high school on their summer trip to France. It was a small high school in a rural area which meant there was more of a family atmosphere amongst the students. The older ones tended to look after the younger ones. The group leader was the venerable Mrs Candelmass. Not only was she liked by all the children, but she was the only person who spoke any French and therefore vital for the trip.

She was an accomplished and experienced teacher who had worked in an assortment of tough Tyneside schools, before coming to the relative idyll of this rural school. During those torrid times she told the story of a boy who was angry and threatened her colleague, shouting, "I'll fetch my father up, I'll fetch my father up. You just watch". The teacher had calmly replied, "Son, I don't care if you fetch your dinner up – you're still on detention." Later on that day the boy came back to school with his father, who proceeded to beat up the teacher.

Mrs Candelmass led the trip and everything ran smoothly until the last night. The final treat for the children was a visit to Euro

Disney (as it was then called). The bus drivers knew it as Euro Misery because things seemed to go wrong there. We spent all day there and Mrs Candelmass had given the children precise instructions to meet back at the bus by a certain time in the evening, so that we could make the 1am ferry at Calais we were booked on.

The temptations and lures of the Magic Kingdom proved too great. Two boys stubbornly stayed inside to watch the nightly Grand parade and firework display. The other children and teachers were waiting on the bus and ready to leave. The gentle Mrs Candelmass started to fume. Two hours later the boys ambled slowly back to the bus, grinning as they went. Mrs Candelmass's patience passed breaking point and she yelled at the two boys in full view of everyone. Their grins vanished. Following one almighty balling out, they had to face an even more unpleasant welcome as they clambered aboard the bus and found their seats. The other children were far from polite as they had been waiting for two hours and were in poor humour.

It seemed a long time since the parents were tearfully waving off their children at the coach park outside the school. The children had been delighted to be leaving and were happy for the first ten miles. Then the girls decided that they missed their boyfriends and the rest of the trip was spent talking or texting on their mobile phones. It was an experience for them, and the teenagers were enthusiastic except when mealtimes came around. Their faces fell when they saw the French food. "What's that then?" they would disapprovingly ask. At each successive meal their reaction was worse and they hardly touched anything. "Urghh, what's that – it's green." "Yes, of course," said the chef. "They're beans."

McDonalds was to save the day. There was visible relief when one was spotted near the hotel in Reims. As soon as dinner was over, where they ate nothing, there was a stampede to be the first to grab a Big Mac.

The French trip had left its mark because ten years later a girl boarded the service bus I was driving on her way to work. "I know you," she said. "I remember you well. You drove us to France when we were at school."

"What did you remember most about the trip?" I asked, "Paris? The Eiffel Tower? Reims Cathedral?"

"No, none of those. But do you remember Mrs Candelmass's amazing outburst at Disney? We were all shocked as we had known her at school for four and a half years but we had never seen her like that. It was wonderful as those boys thoroughly deserved it."

It was my first school trip abroad and I was looking forward to a summer in Europe with many more proposed tours. But it did not turn out that way and the furthest southerly point I reached was Dewsbury. I was sent the day after I returned from France. I came back down to earth with a bump with the return to the loud school teaching staff.

"You'd better be a good driver," said a blunt and buxom Yorkshire classroom assistant. "If you're not I'll be after you," with a wink. The children behind her started to snigger. She turned to face the rear of the bus and shrieked, "Cock off, the lot of you." She turned back to me and reverted to her pouting persona and speaking in a soft voice, "Now, what was I saying?"

It was also a return to the old folks clubs and the mystery tours. I took one group through the wilds of the Northumbrian moorland on what should have been a glorious summer's evening. It turned into an authentic mystery as the fog and mist came down so low that I hadn't a clue where I was going. When we returned to our starting point a very old lady slowly came down the aisle of the bus and was the last to get off. She stopped beside me, leant over and placed a 50p coin into my hands. She stared and said, "Well, dear, you are better than some but not as good as others." Then she turned and walked off.

To this day, I have never decided whether it was meant as a compliment or an insult? Maybe it was a bit of both.

This had been my second job in the bus world. I was beginning to get some experience of buses and life in general. It was 1999, I was about to move into the next stage of my life. Where it would take me, I knew not. One of the company directors, who was scowling as a result of seeing the dent I had just put into his new bus, had a better idea. He gave me an icy stare and growled, "Find the indispensible bus driver and fire him ... and I am going to begin right here."

I did not wait around to see whether he would carry out his threat. Romance beckoned first. That was indispensible, as far as I was concerned.

Caution
Beware of
coach traffic

Ambiguous signs were everywhere. This one could apply to coaches or passengers, both equally dangerous at times.

EMERGENCY USE ONLY

OPEN   CLOSE

The Emergency door buttons were useful when wanting to get drunks and violent passengers off the bus in a hurry.

A stereotypical view of the average bus driver's seat during my rest period.

HOT GASES

Drains were always being sought as likely places for 'dropping the toilet'.

The bus driver's friend – a mop and bucket for cleaning up after a school trip.

Bus spotting on honeymoon in Yerevan, Armenia. Note that though the bus was crude, it was streets ahead of British buses with LPG gas cylinders on roof.

The flyer for the Andy Goldsworthy Travelling Gallery exhibition where I met my wife.

Andy Goldsworth

Leaves, Sand, Sticks, Snow, Ston

Sculptures from the Arctic, Australia, Great Britain, Jap

Cherry Patch yellow to red Kiinagashima - Cho Japan

A Travelling Gallery exhibition tour for
County Durham, Cumbria & Northumberland

16ᵗʰ - 27ᵗʰ June 1998

On the upper deck of the Travelling Gallery which housed all the artworks.

INTERLUDE

I MET MY WIFE ON A DOUBLE-DECKER BUS

The first time I took my new bride on to my bus, it could have been an instant reason for a separation. The raw introduction to my diverse and forthright passengers would have sent many women running. My wife, to a certain degree, was used to it. Her job took her into contact with all types of people so even the lengthy description of someone's health problems did not put her off. On the buses in the North of England, I had found that it was a mistake to ask someone how they were as it tended to result in a long and over-detailed dissertation on their ailments with a rather too graphic tour of their insides.

I broke my own stringent guidelines when I picked up a passenger at a bus stop in the middle of nowhere. He tended to wear the same pair of brown trousers and gave off the strong whiff of badger, ferret, wee-wee and mothballs. As he was the local poacher, there was often a dead rabbit or pheasant located somewhere under his jacket which may have contributed to the overall aroma but not that much.

"How are you?" I asked, breaking my own rules.

He took a deep breath, looked up and down the bus to see who was on before announcing in a loud voice,

"I'm not in good fettle. Not fine fettle at all." He took a deeper breath and stared directly at my wife Pauline before continuing, "I've got a big boil on the inside of my left buttock."

What made the description worse was the fact that he insisted in pronouncing "buttock" as "butt-ock", reminiscent of Forrest Gump telling a fat man on the bench that a bullet had "hit me directly in the butt-ocks". I waited to see if his next remark would be another Gumpism such as, "The only good thing about being wounded in the buttocks is the ice cream."

But it was worse. "The doctor said it was very nasty. So he got a large needle. He jammed it in. And oh what a mess there was ... and ..."

The bus shuddered and I felt the squirming of the other passengers, particularly from my wife, who was sitting in the seat behind me. As words such as "cushion", "infection", "rubber gloves", "oozing", "puss", "stained" and "pants" were spat out, she turned slightly green.

This was like being thrown in at the deep end as I introduced the bus driving element of our new marriage. I needn't have worried as my wife had experienced many unusual antics on buses long before she had met me. As a four year-old (in the days when young children happily travelled on their own) she took the wrong bus. She always followed a group of older schoolgirls, knowing that they boarded the same bus every day which went past her house. On this dark winter's evening, they had unfortunately decided to take a different bus which headed into the city centre. The four-year-old found herself lost in the metropolis and started to cry. But this was 1961. It was a different era where life was more relaxed and an old lady saw her sitting on the pavement crying and came to the rescue. She put her on the right bus and paid the 1d fare so she got home.

Later on in life, she worked for a community arts organisation which worked with people with disabilities. In one group was a particular woman in a wheelchair who on one visit had her leg in plaster.

"How did you do that?" She asked the woman.

"It was terrible," she said. "I was taking the usual bus to the Adult Training Centre and the driver was helping me off. But he had a false arm and it came off and he dropped me and I broke my leg."

With so much common ground on buses it was probably not so surprising that we met on a double-decker bus. It came out of the blue, at a time where I should have been somewhere else and in a place where I never expected to visit or be doing the job I was doing.

The bus company, unknowingly, had set in motion a chain of events which culminated in our chance meeting. We had been having a disagreement over how many hours I should drive. I quite fancied a week's holiday at my old haunt Royal Ascot. They thought I should be driving a bus. A lucrative new job had come in, driving a double-decker bus, with the driver having to be a guide and part-time curator. The double-decker had been converted into a travelling art gallery, which would be touring around the North of England for two weeks.

"It's got your name written all over it," grinned the boss. "You are always saying how much you like art – so now here's your chance." I was determined to hold firm.

"Nothing would induce me to ... there is nothing you can say which will change my mind."

One week later I was sitting in the driver's cab of an aged two-toned green Leyland Atlantean.

From the outside the double-decker seemed to be a normal bus. It had spent most of its life going up and down the main roads into and out of Newcastle, doing service work and transporting commuters. It had been repainted. The original maroon and yellow had been changed to a more countrified green. In its semi-retirement the bus's function had been adapted for community use, being used by groups such as schools and playgroups throughout the North.

But looks could be deceptive and the interior was unexpectedly minimalist. The lower deck had a TV and video player where the luggage rack used to be. The seat behind the driver had remained and now acted like a sofa for people to be able to watch the video. The rear and the top deck had all the seats removed and the windows were covered with white plywood boards which allowed the space to hang pictures.

Even with all these modifications, it still had the feel of a public service vehicle with the chrome railings, the stairs and the corporate fittings which remained. The real give-away was the smell. It still had the aroma of passengers and very stale tobacco smoke.

It was a new idea in England to drive a travelling art gallery to the remoter parts of the land. Scotland had been running its own successful project for many years and had just invested in a brand new bus. The ancient Atlantean I was going to drive was a poor relation, being over twenty years old. It belched black smoke and listed to one side but it was generally a good runner. In its busy past life in the city, it had not experienced the state of rural roads, the sharpness of the corners or the steepness of the hills. An annoying quirk was that it had no fuel gauge on the dashboard. There was no need for one in a city. The fuel tank was filled to the top in the morning which was enough to carry out the day's twelve hour shift and would be refilled ready for the next shift. The driver never had to worry about running out of fuel. Refuelling was always done for him at the depot.

I did not have this luxury. The only way to check how much diesel there was left was to dip a long stick into the fuel tank. Behind my driver's seat I carried an old walking stick which looked as if it had been ebonised as a result of the diesel staining. As the fuel consumption never rose above 8 miles per gallon, I would stop and nervously dip the tank at regular intervals, especially following a long and arduous climb.

The artist chosen for the travelling exhibition was Andy Goldsworthy.

"You've never heard of Andy Goldsworthy?" was the startled cry from the organiser, who looked stunned then nearly fainted at my ignorance which I am sure marked me out as a philistine.

When we arrived at different venues and I was introduced to supporters as 'the man who had never heard of Andy Goldsworthy.' Everybody seemed to have heard of Andy, except me. His pictures were ephemeral works using nature and he created sculptures out of ice, leaves, water – basically anything he could find in the wild. He would then take a photograph and the sculpture would then be left to disintegrate and return to nature. It was these photographs which I was transporting onboard the double-decker. They were worth thousands of pounds. The whole collection was worth in excess of £50,000.

My education about the artist was rapid. At the end of the two weeks I was an expert. The video ran on a loop whenever the bus was parked. After one day I could repeat every line; after two days I could hum the background music, after the third I had mastered the timing and tones of the accompanying Buddhist bell chimes and after day four I could mimic Andy's voice and accent. In fact by the end of the tour, I felt that I knew him intimately.

With such a valuable cargo of pictures onboard, it meant the bus had to be locked up in a secure compound, I came across a hidden world visiting an assortment of council depots, police stations, auction marts, haulage companies and other bus depots. I parked next to the gritters in Penrith, the cattle wagons in Longtown, the armoured cars in Berwick Barracks and even unmarked articulated trucks filled with millions of pounds-worth of cigarettes at a well known security company depot. Each time the double-decker caused fascination and hundreds of people would appear from all corners and stare at this unusual vehicle in their parking lot.

The Atlantean proved to be an awkward bus to drive over narrow hillside roads, partially because it connected with the many low branches, but more relevantly I found there were an increasing number of bruises being added to my scalp. Each bump would test the light springs and I was catapulted out of my seat, vertically into the ceiling. It was such a painful experience that I had to change my driving style, to something which was similar to a bareback bronco rider, as I stood up, out of the seat as much as I could.

Occasionally the bus would return to the bus company's depot which caused great amusement amongst the fitters, followed by consternation. The bus was too big and looked as if it might not fit under the main doors. They were already nervous, given my track record of having hit the doors before with another double-decker,which nearly put out the front upper deck window. The mechanics dropped everything and raced to find some ladders. I had to inch the bus, in reverse, into the depot whilst the men on stepladders checked the clearance under the door. Halfway in there was a light popping noise followed by many shrieks and yells as the roof of the double decker connected with the door. A solution was found by chance. When the bus was driven into the depot forwards, for some unknown reason it did not connect with the doors. No one could say why or how, but it worked.

On one of the days the bus was booked by the Arts Officer at a council in County Durham, to park up and spend half a day outside a library. The library was in a town near where Tony Blair was the constituency MP. It was a quiet backwater situated a little way on the main street away from the shops. I had just set up the bus and started the Goldsworthy video rolling when a passing pedestrian said she would love to come on to the bus, but she couldn't because she had her dog and dogs were not allowed on the bus. So I offered to hold the dog on the lead outside the bus.

As I stood in the drizzle dog-minding, along the pavement came this beautiful woman with long flowing blonde hair wearing a fashionable olive green long skirt and green jacket. She was bronzed owing to having just returned from a beach in Turkey which heightened the attraction as it brought out the freckles on her nose. This turned out to be the Arts Officer for Sedgefield.

I have many things to thank the dog I was holding on to for. He ran across the entrance of the bus and barred her way, making it impossible for her to board the bus. Standing, looking useless holding this stubborn dog in the doorway of the bus, we started talking. There was nothing else to do. So we talked, and we talked, and we talked some more.

Six months later we were engaged.

One year later we were married in the Lake District. If love was a card game then fate had dealt its hand. Of course we should have never met. Pauline had been snowed under with work. I was going to be at Ascot. But somehow all that changed and at the last moment she decided to take a half-hour break from the office and go to see the Goldsworthy exhibition.

Our wedding was romantic. Our honeymoon could have ended in divorce before we boarded the plane at Heathrow Airport. My new wife looked up at the destination board with anticipation, wondering where the surprise destination would be. She read down the list. Montego Bay? Nairobi? Marrakesh? Bangkok? Worryingly her eyes rested on the final name on the board – Yerevan.

"Darling, where is Yerevan?" she said nervously. "It's the only place I can't place."

That was when her face fell. The dawning realisation of a honeymoon being spent somewhere she knew nothing about was disturbing. But it was too late to turn back so that's where we went.

Even in the backwaters of Armenia, it was impossible not to be reminded of the bus world. Apart from the lovely views out of the hotel window of a distant and snow capped Mount Ararat and getting to know my new wife, there were unusual sights of buses. If my fellow bus drivers had seen me they may have thought that I was behaving like a repressed bus spotter.

I developed a fascination with the succession of Armenian buses rattling along the street. They were all listing at a 45-degree angle and belched acrid black smoke. On their roofs were rows of gas cylinders, precariously tied together with something that looked suspiciously like binder twine and allowed freedom of movement. Looks can however be deceptive, however and Armenia was streets ahead of the UK by running their buses on LPG. Though it was a primitive system, it worked. Our guide told us that the technology was improving and that the number of buses exploding was in decline.

"They only go boom, a few times a year now," he said optimistically.

We crossed the border into Georgia and Tbilisi, where my bus spotting tendencies did not subside. The standard of buses was slightly better. The problem was the state of the roads. One day we noticed a frantic wave of activity as the potholes on the road were hurriedly patched up by an army of workmen. Without warning our bus was moved over to the side of the road by the police with all the other traffic on the road. There we waited until a Soviet style motorcade of sinister, sturdy looking black limousines with darkened windows flew past. It was the, then, President, Edward Shevardnaze and his entourage off to visit a town or village.

"We like him to come and visit our village as it is the only time we get the roads fixed. He is a popular man and everyone wants him," said the bus driver. It was no wonder the roads were cleared as there had been two assassination attempts on the leader in the previous four years; the last being an attack on his motorcade with grenade launchers and machine guns, killing a bodyguard. But the delay had its plus points as it was the perfect excuse for the Georgians to get off the bus, open many bottles of wine and return to the custom in the Caucasus of toasting everyone and everything with the aid of long and mournful poetry.

When they discovered we were British, it became an excuse to elongate the toasts and in progressively slurred voices and produce long eulogies to "Vinston Churcheel", "Bobbie Moooer" "Margitte Datcher" and "Dony Bliar". More bottles were opened.

On return to the bus depot in England my desire to stare at buses subsided, to my wife's relief. She was beginning to wonder whether a busman's holiday and a honeymoon were the same. The boss's wife reinforced this when she told Pauline that she also had difficulty diverting her husband, who was mesmerised by the fast manoeuvres of the Croatian bus drivers on a holiday in Dubrovnik.

On returning home, there was a parcel under the dustbin next to the front doorstep. It contained our most unusual wedding present, a scale model made by Raymond, a fellow driver. It was housed in a vintage red and blue upturned plastic fish tank which acted as the frame. Through the clear Perspex was a two-toned green double-decker bus parked under a tree outside a building which was the library where we met. In front of the bus were two plastic model figures, adjacent to the front doors. One was holding a dog on a lead.

Raymond had been driving trucks and buses for many years and was now then in his late seventies. He had survived a terrifying experience as he was travelling down the main road to the Lakes on the service bus, when the cable which held the spare wheel in place under the bus had snapped. The resulting effect was that the wheel became snagged between the bus and the road. The bus began to act like a turntable as the spare wheel was turning the vehicle from left to right with the driver having no control whatsoever.

Raymond wrote in his statement to the boss afterwards, "We were at some forty-five degrees off course heading towards the cars coming up the hill ... the whole coach rocked from side to side ... I was now heading straight into the side of the caravan ... and I watched fascinated as the caravan leapt a yard into the air after plunging over a culvert."

All this was happening at 50mph. The friction heated up the spare wheel and it became so hot that eventually exploded. This was a good thing as the driver maintained control of the bus and was able to safely bring it to a halt in a side road.

"The fear of fire," went on Raymond, "got my weakened knees to push the seat back ... I could hear in the silence, someone sobbing quietly in the back of the coach..." It was a close run thing.

I frequently look at the model Raymond made. It still makes me smile at the absurdity of the chance of meeting one's wife in such an unlikely place, and I often think of of Robin's words – "I know in those last few seconds before we started to roll, it was providence. Ask my passengers."

I thought – ask my wife. Was it providence that brought us together?

CHAPTER 5

THE AMERICANS HAVE LANDED

Having set the scene of my introduction to bus driving, from childhood to marriage and introducing some of the characters I found myself surrounded by, there was one area of the job which I adored with a passion. That was when it came to transporting the Americans around this country.

The British perception of the American tourist hasn't changed much over the years. The average British bus driver's view has remained the same. Though the world had changed, the drivers I spoke to thought that the behaviour, the comments and the outlook of the average American on a bus tour of the British Isles was the same as it ever was.

"They're crackers, man," said one north-eastern driver.

In parts, I had to agree with him.

I had grown up with the stereotypical view of an American tourist by watching films. Unbelievably when I started driving American tours, the stereotypes came to life. I met several like Sherriff J.W. Pepper (the loud Sherriff who appeared in some of the James Bond films). All of the Golden Girls had been on. So too had, it appeared, most of the cast from The Love Boat, Scrubs, Lost, National Lampoon and The Big Bang Project. Eddie Murphy, Richard Pryor and Leslie Nielsen clones were never far away. I tried to avoid making comparisons, but it was impossible not to and I invariably had to suppress my natural desire to say something like, "You look so like ... you behave like ... you speak exactly like John Doe in the film ..."

As a race, we seem to have always loved to hear stories of downright stupidity from Americans, like the passenger who was landing at Heathrow, who turned to his neighbour as they flew over Windsor Castle and said, "That architect who built that castle so near the airport, should be shot." Or like the man who asked if that famous writer Fort William was still alive. Why? It detracts from our own inadequacies I suppose and gives us British a sense of superiority.

It was a guessing game I employed to pass the time, as I waited for the next inbound American tour in the coach bay outside the terminal at Glasgow Airport. What would they be like? The fantasy never lived up to the reality and I always seemed to draw the short straw. Other drivers had described the buses being filled with Californian bronzed, blonde beauties straight out of the cheerleading team and preppy men looking as if they had walked out of the pages of a Lands End or L.L. Bean catalogue. As I stared at an incoming group, struggling along the eroded pavements with their vast suitcases on wheels and wobbling bodies bouncing along, it dawned on me that my fellow drivers must have been pulling my leg.

This tour moved with purpose towards my bus and stopped by the open entry door.

The largest lady in the lead leant in, looked me up and down, and sniffed before saying, "Don't just sit there, bus driver. Get our bags on to the bus." The tour guide, who was following directly behind looked at me sorrowfully and her eyes rolled about, pleading with me to do what the teacher had asked. I meekly complied.

They were a school from somewhere in the Mid-West. The children were uninterested in more or less everything except for the odd neon sign we travelled by which advertised some American franchise or product. The big yellow arched M on a red background caused spontaneous applause and a desire to chomp on a double cheeseburger before having to face, what they perceived to be, the dreaded British food.

"We've been warned," said the teacher.

The teachers all wore thick horn-rimmed glasses. Some were purple, others were deep red. The head teacher wore a different pair every day and had gone through the range of primary colours before departing for home. The tour was dour for the first few days. I found them obtuse and in their own words they "couldn't give a damn". They were hating every minute of it. Each morning, my heart would sink as I descended the hotel staircase and had to sit amongst them at breakfast. Each morning, it was the same, the same complaints, the same drawling whines.

"Where's the grits?" they would shout at the mouse-like Scottish waitress. "Haven't you got Heinz ketchup? I've never heard of this make. I can't eat this disgusting sausage without it." The head teacher weighed in, "Waitress. Where's the goddamn waitress. Where can you find a waitress around here? This service stinks ... ah, AT LAST. Haven't you got decaf? I asked for decaf ...", and so it went on, every breakfast; every lunch; every tea and dinner. The guide would cringe, the waitresses would cringe and I would cringe. They were unhappy about everything. Nothing was right. I had to take out my frustrations somewhere; enough was enough.

My solution was that I became mischievous. I had remembered hearing another driver saying that he adored Americans because you could tell them anything and nine times out of ten they would believe it. Like the time he had been standing by the side of Loch Ness when one of the men on the tour came up to him and asked him, "See here Donald. Have you seen the Loch Ness monster?"

"Yes, I married her," he replied with a deadpan face.

"Oh really?" said the shocked American and he walked slowly away shaking his head, willing to believe it yet not sure how to cope with the age old tradition of English sarcasm and irony.

I began inserting some outlandish comments and nuggets of clearly false information into our conversations. None of them registered anything other than sour looks and replies. I was about to give up, when one morning a miracle happened. The whole group were standing at the foot of the Wallace Monument near Stirling and for some reason I thought it would be a good idea to namedrop and let slip that my mother's family were Wallaces. The group unexpectedly became animated with excitement and enthusiasm.

"Say. Are you a descendant of William Wallace?"

"Well yes and no," I replied, which was a half truth and the whole truth could be blamed on the fact that the history of Wallace had become a little murky in the mists of time, that though it was 90% certain that I was no direct descendent, the 10% element of doubt was allowable. Realistically, the best I could hope for was that I was a very distant relative. Most historians seemed to rely heavily on the poems of Blind Harry as the official history, but they were written two hundred years after Wallace's death and could never be described as truly accurate.

That did not deter me from embellishing my family history with the Americans, particularly when the very mention of *Braveheart* sent them into a tizzy and they fell over each other, reaching for their cameras.

"I do not believe my luck," said the boorish head teacher. "I'm in the presence of a genuine Wallace." I felt like Royalty. They snuggled up to me and fluttered their eyelashes and smiled for the first time since the trip began. "Say do you mind if we take a photo of you standing with us?"

From that moment on the atmosphere changed. They were fun and the tour became a pleasure. I did not have the inclination to risk going back to the bad days by telling them the truth about my not so blue blood.

"Are you his grandson?" asked one of the younger members of the group? I did not have the heart to tell him that if I was William Wallace's grandson, I would be around 652 years old. Ignorance was bliss.

From then on, my attitude changed. I looked forward to the tours with relish. Most were interested in the UK and wanted to learn. They were also the most generous tippers. The tours were hard work and they all brought jumbo sized suitcases with them which had to be lugged all over the place. If the hotel reception was on the second floor, as it sometimes was, it would be backbreaking work carrying fifty extra large items of luggage.

The bus company had tried to pull a fast one on one of the tours. They had run out of buses. All the larger, 53 and 57-seaters were out on other jobs. All that was left was a small 11-metre Volvo.

"I can't take that," a driver called Donald had told the boss, "it won't be big enough for all their cases."

"Don't worry about it," the boss had said. "everything will be just fine. You'll get them in somehow."

On arrival at the port, everything was far from fine. Only half the cases fitted in the lockers below. The passengers had to sit on the seats with suitcases on their knees. The back seats and the aisles were crammed with luggage. Donald tried to pacify the irate tour guide, but it was no good and another bus from another company was summonsed. It was an expensive morning.

The groups came from all over the USA. They came from different states and demonstrated the differences in dialect, food and culture. The only common factor seemed to be the identical size and weight of their suitcases.

Occasionally there were the odd acts of crass stupidity, ignorance and stubbornness. On another tour, as we were meandering through the Yorkshire country lanes through the beautiful countryside on a Herriot Country Tour, the large gentleman in the seat behind me gave a large sigh and said, "Why don't they widen the roads around here? We'd get there a lot quicker."

His grouchiness continued for the whole tour. He was an awkward sod who complained about everything. He was nasty, a bully who no one liked. He was potentially dangerous, too, as he constantly threatened to sue everybody who had done the smallest thing wrong.

He was accompanied by his wife who seemed to be in fear of his outbursts the whole time and hence was a mouse-like creature, who rarely opened her mouth. When she did, she agreed with everything he said. She never laughed, rarely smiled and seemed to lack any form of confidence. The only time I did see her smile was when this obese idiot got his comeuppance on the banks of Lake Windermere, when he bent over a little too far to look more closely at some ducks and the law of physics took over making sure he went in head first. Not only was this in front of the coach party, but a great many other tourists were promenading along the shores on this lovely Sunday afternoon. Everyone, at first, suppressed their giggles as this enraged figure strode around the shallows like a rhino disturbed from his water hole. He was apoplectic with rage and as great fortune would have it, turned on the first person he saw, who happened to be a park warden.

This was a big mistake.

The park warden, as he told me quietly later, had just been sent on an anger management course and knew exactly how to deal with angry individuals such as this. She took the safe option and called the police, who reacted to the perceived threat with vigour. When there was a disturbance which involved a bus, they tended to err on the side of caution, as they did in this case and arrived with a van containing four policemen, closely followed by two other squad cars for backup. Little did they know that they were coming up against a veteran who had served with Special Forces in Vietnam in his younger days, as he liked to constantly remind the tour group.

He flattened the first two policemen who approached him. The others jumped on him and it took all six officers to hold him down on the ground, while one policemen struggled to put the handcuffs on. But the American's wrists were too big and they had to resort to binding him with rope before frogmarching him away.

That was the last I saw of him. He never came back on the bus. Nor did his wife. She was still quiet as she followed her husband into the police van. Later we heard that he had been given a caution and had flown home.

Without him, the atmosphere lightened and the group came out of their shells and began to tell stories of home. A couple from Texas said they thought that the angry man may have come from Montana where they thought strange things tended to happen. The last time they had been there the Texan said, it had been on a hunting trip.

"Hillbilly country," he said "The farmers there go out on the eve of the hunting season with pots of pink paint, painting in large letters:

C O W

on their pedigree stock, so that they would not be shot by short-sighted or overenthusiastic hunters."

At the end of the day, he had been waiting in line at the game warden's desk, which was sited next to the entrance to the park. All kills had to be presented before they were allowed to be taken home. Another hunter with thick spectacles queue barged and walked in front of him dragging a donkey. The wardens did not have the heart to tell him that it was not the deer he was so insistent he had shot.

"So maybe now do you understand why this hillbilly behaved like he did and made all our lives a misery?" said the Texan, as we both watched the police van disappear around the corner.

* * * * *

The most interesting was the top end of the market, which was run by some of the world's biggest tour companies. The customers tended to be retired captains of industry and the wealthy. Their 14-day tour of Britain would cost upwards of $8,000, which would mean that they were even more discerning customers, criticising the minutest mistake or thing that they felt was not up to standard. They were mainly elderly, though sometimes they were accompanied by teenage children or grandchildren who would look bored and take the first available chance to escape to the nightclubs.

I liked their directness. Sometimes there would be praise when things had gone well. "Good job, Tom!" someone would yell out as I missed hitting an oncoming vehicle coming hurtling round the corner for the fifteenth time that day.

They generally had a good sense of humour, though the nuances and eccentricities of British jokes went over their heads and I would see them standing there in puzzlement trying to work out the punchline or whether I was just pulling their legs.

"This town was once inhabited by a group of green eyed tourists from Mars who beamed down one afternoon and were seen having a picnic by the river," I would say and wait for the standard reply ...

"You are kidding."

"No it's true," I'd reply. "Shakespeare wrote about it in Macbeth."

"Oh, really? You don't say."

It was a bus driver's only way of mounting a harmless defence and a chance for payback time when someone had been unpleasant or a situation could be defused with some gentle teasing. To completely destroy any faith they had in me, I would turn to my fellow driver and say in a loud voice: "I haven't driven this bus before. In fact I've only been driving for two days. Can you tell me what this pedal does – is it the brake by any chance." The tourists in the seat behind would turn white and summon the tour guide, who would in turn expand on the bad driver theme if he, too, did not like the tour group.

The service in Britain seemed to be a major disappointment to the Americans.

The larger tour companies realised this and circumvented these shortcomings by bringing their own American tour guides with them, who understood the needs of their American passengers and how to deal with their complaints. They were professional and as a bus driver I found that a close relationship developed where each depended on the other. Benton, was one of the most experienced, who would work from May to October before retiring for the winter to some beach in Mexico, where he said the only decision he had to make was what colour shorts he was going to wear when he got up in the morning. The following spring Benton would be back in the UK, guiding again. At the beginning of the season he would look amazingly fit, healthy and be full of energy, like a sun tanned film star, fresh off the beach. As the season progressed, he became more weary looking, more haggard and dispirited as summer turned to autumn.

This was the pattern with most of the guides as the pressure was a constant weight of being on hand nearly 24 hours a day, problem solving and managing to keep smiling when they were being scolded for some wrong.

The passengers tested Benton's patience to the limit. There was the 25 stone man who would board the bus, fall asleep by the first corner and snore loudly. The passengers became irritated by this as they could not hear Benton's witty and informative commentary over the noise. A young girl found the secret to stopping him. She said she had noticed that whenever Benton would say "picture stop", "sightseeing stop" or "meal break", the man would wake up, jump up from his seat and head for the door as fast as he could. So for the rest of the time, whenever the snoring started, he would yell "meal break" into the microphone and there would be a thrashing sound as the man would struggle to get out of his seat. It worked every time.

The passengers' irritation quickly turned to hatred of this man, particularly as at every meal he would race for the buffet counter, pushing the others out of the way. He then proceeded to pile his plate so high with food that there was little left for the others when they got there. Something had to give.

It did, on the last day of the tour in a pub in London. He did his usual trick. He ran to the table where all the food was laid out, slobbering at the mouth as he knocked over those standing in line. He piled his plate sky high and smugly retired to sit in a crescent shaped wooden chair.

To the others joy, the legs of the chair gave way. Yet the middle part of the chair had attached itself to his midriff. He struggled up off the floor and walked around the room like a wild bull desperately trying to free himself from the remains of the chair. "Oh how sweet revenge is," one of the younger members on the tour announced.

Benton seemed to have the answer to most things and was always able to find the most appropriate put-downs. One woman complained the whole time about anything and everything. On the final day she came running on to the bus and whined, "Oh Benton, Benton, what can I do today?"

"Well," he replied unemotionally, "you can start by going up to the hotel receptionist and complain to her as you have done to all the other hotel receptionists on the previous thirteen days." The woman was speechless, but caused no more trouble.

One of the guides I came across was not pleasant to drive for. Not only did he easily lose his temper and berate the drivers, but he also used to brag about how wonderful he was. He led us to believe that he was god's gift to women. Other drivers, when they saw him, would try to run in the opposite direction. This changed when he was given the shock of his life by a group of American nurses on his tour.

As he was relaxing, sitting on the bar stool in the pub one evening, one of the girls asked him if he would go to the bus and retrieve her jersey. He did so and as he was searching for the garment he was pushed to the floor by the girls who had crept on to the bus via the emergency exit. The guide was stripped, tied up and left naked on the front seat. They released him shortly afterwards, but not before the word had got around and all the hotel staff and other guests, who equally disliked him, had walked past the bus.

The next morning, at breakfast, there was no sign of the guide. He vanished. The tour was three hours late as a replacement had to be found and transported from the head office.

"Hell hath no fury like an American nurse," said the driver. "I entertained no nurse fantasies ever again but I could have hugged them for getting rid of the guide."

I drove other varied groups from different states. The Iowa farmers came and went with a bang, singing their favourite song, 'Throw Grandmother Off The Bus'. On another trip, the bus was filled with one family; the Stewart family had booked the whole tour.

"We've come to trace our ancestor" – a familiar tale from many Americans.

"And who is your ancestor?" asked the guide.

"Why, Bonnie Prince Charlie, of course." This was normal. The majority of Americans claimed they were visiting to trace their Scottish or Irish roots. It is a case of the pot calling the kettle black when I am guilty of doing the same thing with my Wallace ancestry.

"Can you tell me the way to the Beatrix Potteries? I want to buy some cups," another member of the Stewart family asked as we were touring the Lake District, naively mistaking the museum to the famous childrens' author for a craft shop. It was a similar mix-up to what happened to a friend's father was walking down the street in Stratford-upon-Avon in his capacity as a consultant for the local tourist board, when an American tourist barred his way and asked:

"Excuse me. Is this the way to the manger?"

"The manger? The manger? I can't think of any manger anywhere near ..." my friend's father replied rather puzzled, before a light bulb lit up inside his head and he realised what was being requested: "Oh I see now. NO there's no manger here – this is Stratford-upon-Avon. This is Shakespeare's birthplace, not Jesus's."

I became involved with another American top end tour company by chance. It was a case of being in the right place at the right time. A bus company based near London rang the boss at the depot to ask if they could supply a relief driver one day a week so that the regular driver could have his legally required rest period. I was one of the lucky drivers. The first time was a nerve-wracking experience as the previous three drivers from the company had driven into a very narrow bridge and damaged the bus.

I felt the pressure was on. One more dent and they might never use us again. I arrived early at the hotel in the Lake District, noticing that the entrance was not only narrow but the driveway was lined with boulders. In the first 20 seconds after departing, I had belted a boulder and put a scratch mark into one of the side panels. I spent the rest of the day trying to think how I was going to explain this and the only consolation I could see, was that I was carrying on the tradition of my driver colleagues. The first few minutes were terrifying as we headed to Ambleside over tiny roads with stone walls on either side. Around every corner flew a local and smoke was visible as they jammed on their brakes and came to a halt a few feet from the front of the bus leaving rubber skid marks on the road.

The atmosphere became even more tense. There were sharp and audible intakes of breath from the doubly nervous passengers, sitting behind. In between the sound of the sucking of teeth, whistling, there was one voice which kept saying, "Jeeeeeeeezzzzzussh christ. Sheeeiiitt that was close. Good job, Tom."

After the initial shock, it became fractionally more fun and though every corner was a challenge it was satisfying when completed without incident. The tour went through Ambleside, stopping at the Lake for a picture stop before going on to Bowness on Lake Windermere, where they had a couple of hours in the tourist friendly town. The drive continued down to the foot of the lake, then across to Lake Coniston.

I went so often that I began to memorise the guide's spiel, which rarely altered. "Now here are the Herdwick sheep – distinguishable because they always look as if they are smiling," or "Do you know how the farmers count sheep, in their Cumbrian. It's Yan, Tyan, Tethera, Methera, Pimp......Dick......Bumfit ......Giggot" by the time he reached 20 there were reams of applause. It never failed. John Ruskin was always well discussed: "He was a great man – his motto was: There's no wealth but life" and when Ruskin's great love was mentioned the guide would make a dramatic pause before divulging her name: "She was called Rose La Touche", at which again the bus would descend into sniggers. And as we passed a school, next door to a pub, next to a church, the guide would become animated in preparation for the appreciation of his joke and say: "Remember it is education followed by temptation followed by salvation." There were nods of agreement.

In Coniston there was a right turn down to the pier from which the Gondola, a restored Victorian pleasure steamer departed. Halfway down this road there was a narrow stone bridge followed by a sharp right-hander. It looked innocent as I drove over it.

However when it came to going back over it, it proved atrociously difficult to negotiate. There was no room for error, as had been already demonstrated by the three buses which had already been scraped. The group left to take a boat across the lake and see Ruskin's house, Brantwood. I sat in the bus, wondering how I was going to get over this infernal bridge. I went to look at it three times, trying to visualise the angles and correct approach. Finally the time came to try and with inches to spare, aided by a lot of intakes of the normal breath and teeth sucking behind me, I made it.

"Good job, Tom," said the guide over the microphone.

"Good job, Tom" echoed around the bus. I was just relieved it was all over.

Chapter 5

The tour continued around even windier roads, where faster traffic flew round every corner. Past the celebrated house where people sunbathed topless in their garden, under the misconception that the hedge gave them protection from any prying eyes. Appalling timing meant that they were always in the nude as our busload of Americans passed. One day, as I was driving past, they realised for the first time that they were being watched and hurriedly ran into their house, clutching any piece of exposed modesty. The passengers cheered. From that day on, I have never seen the garden door open, let alone anyone sitting in the garden.

When we arrived at the hotel, there was the regular driver, much relieved to have his bus back in one piece. The dent didn't worry him as it was the minimum amount of damage he had seen to his returned bus when compared to what some the other drivers managed to do.

The more I acted as the relief driver, the more I got to know and love the Lake District. I became friendly with the guides, the café owners, the boatmen and the curators. I would listen to what they told the American tourists as I tacked on to the back of the tour. It helped me once, when I arrived to drive the bus on a frosty autumn morning to receive a surprise. The regular driver was unusually in his uniform. I had always seen him in his casual clothes before as it was his day off. Something was wrong. This time he took me directly to the guide's bedroom. The curtains were drawn and she was lying on top of her bed in her pyjamas and dressing gown. From beneath a wet flannel positioned over her face, came moans and groans. She was suffering from a bug or food poisoning. She said it was impossible for her to move and that I had to act as tour guide for the day – the regular driver would drive.

And that's what I did. I repeated the spiels of the various other guides I had listened to, word for word. I was able to make some comment or other as we passed the notable spots. The Rose La Touche joke came tumbling out, pausing for effect and waiting for the usual tittering. As did all the other old faithfuls. Yan, Tyan, Tethera, Methera, Pimp. I had listened to so much over the summer months. It was a fun day and the tip was good. Little did I know it was the last tour I would do.

The next week another driver went over to drive and had an altercation with a Land Rover. The lovely new Setra bus was dented to such an extent that it was close to being deemed a write-off. The result was that it was the final nail in the coffin, as far as me and my colleagues were concerned. The next season, the telephone remained ominously silent with no requests for a relief driver.

I enjoyed driving at the other end of the American tours scale – there was a holiday tour company known by the bus company drivers as 'Effing Tours', possibly because of the long hours and hard graft. Effing Tours kept their prices down by putting their customers into lower grade hotels and using the cheaper bus companies. Some of the vehicles which transported these Americans could only be described as rust buckets. They were hard nosed business people, known in the industry for paying a middling rate, but some bus companies were caught out by the small print, which made them liable for all parking charges and dead mileage between tours, which effectively wiped out most of the profit. Amazingly they had plenty of operators knocking at their door who wanted the work.

Effing was an unusual company. This was because of the guides were mainly students on a gap year, who had travelled the world and done a variety of jobs. Some had been election counters in Bosnia, others were graduates with jobs like political researcher or activist, some were actors and some couldn't figure out what they wanted to do in life. All bar one were interesting.

Algernonwas rude, churlish and had and a nervous disposition. I took an instant dislike to him and could not wait for the tour to end. Through my own stupidity, I inadvertently nearly ended the tour early. It was while we stopped in Stratford-upon-Avon for the afternoon. Having dropped off the guide and the tour party in the middle of the town, I decided against sitting in the coach park for four hours and having to pay a hefty fee to park my bus. Instead I had what I thought was the inspired idea of driving out to Stratford Racecourse, where there was an enormous free car park as it was not a race day and bound to be empty.

For me it was also an indulgent trip down memory lane to a place where I had worked when I was in the horseracing world in the past. To pass the time and to loosen up following the drive from London I walked round the track. It was mid-summer. The grass had been allowed to grow because a good covering of grass cushioned the horses' hooves as they galloped over the firm ground. So good was the covering that it must have reached a height of 8-10 inches.

The warm July sunshine made me feel more human again and the time sped by. As my watch indicated there was less than an hour until I was due to pick up the guide and the Americans, I felt in my pocket for the keys to the bus. No keys. I checked the other pockets. Still no keys. I checked everything. Absolutely no sign of any keys whatsoever.

Panic rising, I rang the office to seek advice. Bemused they said: "Nothing we can do. You'll have to ring Volvo." Volvo were equally unimpressed and said everyone went home early on a Friday and nothing could be done until Monday morning. I felt sick. I was soon going to have to ring the guide with the nervous disposition and tell him, in the gentlest possible way that the tour was over for now or until the keys could be found.

The tour looked doomed.

A replacement bus, if there was one available would have to be despatched. This wouldn't get here until at least 2am. A fat lot of good for the Americans who had an action packed evening planned. The chance of them making the RSC performance of The Tempest later that evening was looking remote. Alternatively a local bus company, if they were available would have to be contracted. Either way it would cost the bus company a small fortune, eating away Effing Tours' meagre profit and moreover plunging it deep into the red. There would be anger all around. I was firmly in the doghouse.

I tried retracing my steps. But 1½ miles of thick grass is a tall order and looking for a needle in a haystack would be comparatively easier. Some Alsatians from the Police Dog Unit happened to be training with their handlers up the final furlong of the racecourse. The handlers thought it was the best story they had heard all year. They offered to send their dogs out to try and find the keys. For a moment there was hope as the dogs searched under the running rails. But they turned out to be hopeless, preferring to hang around their handlers in the hope of a snack.

So I headed back to the bus in the lowest spirits, thinking how I was going to break the news to Algernon. It would not be an enviable experience. As I picked up my mobile phone and started dialing the number, a glint of metal in a ditch near the car park, caught my eye. I bent down expecting to find an old Coke tin, but it turned out to be the keys.

I grabbed my phone and punched in the number.

"Hello," said the nervous voice on the other end of the line.

"I'll be with you in 10 minutes." I said as calmly as I could.

"Great" he replied and disconnected. It must have been a million – no a ten million to one chance of finding the keys.

The Americans boarded the bus at the due time. No one was any the wiser. The passengers had had their fill of Shakespeare. The guide seemed happy – that was until I told him. Of course I had to tell him. I couldn't resist it. It was pretty obvious what his reaction would be. It proved to be better than I had ever hoped as the blood visibly drained from his face before he keeled over in the courier seat and hit his head on the chrome door handle.

It was a peaceful trip thereafter and the guide had little to say and tried his hardest to avoid me, which was difficult when driver and guide had to sit on adjacent seats at the front of the bus.

Effing Tours was the bargain basement mainly for schools from all round the USA. They did whistle-stop tours around Europe. Europe in four days. Then they would arrive in London and do the UK in 3 days. Day 1 – London to Oxford – drive in and out of the main gate at Blenheim Palace – Stratford-upon-Avon – Coventry late after a play at the RSC. Day 2 Coventry – Grasmere – flying visit to Rydal Mount – Gretna or Moffat Woollen Mill – Edinburgh. Day 3 – Edinburgh. Day 4 , 3am Edinburgh to Glasgow Airport and fly home.

The student guides would give a brief talk as we travelled. They were different from the guides from the more upmarket companies I had been used to. Things happened in a more haphazard way and they spent much time trying to find places where commission could be made and sometimes split with the driver. Most boat operators, woollen mills, eateries, would be only too delighted to receive a coach load and would offer nice incentives to drivers and guides. One of the best money earners was shortbread. In the coach parks across the country I saw drivers returning to their buses unable to see in front of them because of the number of tartan tins they carried. One colleague told me that a good driver on a 10-day coach tour would expect to make £1500-£2000 in commission.

Remember this was before the millennium. Times have changed and it is not so easy to do this these days.

My final Effing Tour ended up at Stirling Castle. There in the coach park was a Scottish driver called Hector, who I had met before and had been on the driving circuit for many years. He had just had a life changing experience and had met his wife in extraordinary circumstances.

Hector, like all drivers, met many women on the tours he drove. On this particular tour he met a 22 year-old from Canada. They got on famously, in a platonic way. Though Hector was much older, when he dropped off the tour and said farewell to the girl they both agreed that it had been a happy time but he thought no more about it and went straight on to his next tour to Ireland.

Halfway round, disaster struck as somehow he fell out of the back of the bus, down the steps, on to the metal road and broke his collar bone. He was flown home to Glasgow by the company. When he arrived at Glasgow Airport, once he had collected his bag, Hector sat down, feeling sorry for himself with feeling miserable and in pain.

He heard a voice and looked up to see the Canadian girl standing in front of him. She had decided on the homeward journey that she missed Hector and could not bear to be without him. Taking a gamble, she had caught the next flight back to Glasgow to look for him. In a romantic coincidence they both arrived at the airport terminal at the same time. His destiny was mapped out in an instant. They were married shortly after.

The last time I said goodbye to an Effing Tour, I stood by the bus and I waved to the large teacher in the multi-coloured horn rimmed glasses as she tried to enter the departure lounge in Edinburgh airport. As she walked into the glass revolving doors there was a collision and loud noise as the automatic mechanism came to an abrupt halt.

"Goddamn shitface lousy limey motherfuckin' doors", echoed around the concourse. The nice deputy teacher turned to me and laughed:

"I'm a good American, but when she's around, I often lie and say I'm from Canada."

I opened the brown envelope with the tip they had given me. It was filled with a sizeable amount of dollars. Attached was a note which read – "You come over and see us when you are over, you hear". I regret I never did.

That was the last time I was going to transport Americans for quite some time. My recent marriage meant I was moving to Whitley Bay, on the Tyneside coast. It was too far to commute to the bus company at the top of the hill, so I had to look for another company to drive for. The companies I looked at in this more industrial part of Northumberland had a different clientele.

"Don't go there," warned my old boss. "It's the Wild West."

"They speak in a funny accent and tell odd jokes," said another driver "like ... there's been a crash on the road and a load of amphibians have spilt on to the road ... it's a turtle disaster ... or the woman who went into the hairdresser and asked, "Will you do me a perm?" ... "why certainly, pet," she replied. "I wandered lonely as a cloud..."

I knew little about the area. It seemed to be the location of F.A. Cup giant killing soccer teams such as Blyth Spartans and legendary players such as Wor Jackie (Jackie Milburn), Bobby and Jackie Charlton. It was still reputed to be one of the main recruitment areas for the parachute regiment. It had a reputation of being a tough place.

But to a contrarian like me, it seemed the right place to drive buses, however tough its reputation was. I was soon going to find out. Based on past performances, no doubt the accidental part of my bus driving would not disappear and things were bound to happen.

Sending the Americans across Lake Coniston on the launch.

Waiting to board the Gondola on the crowded Coniston jetty.

The coach park in the Lake District had a novel way of saving money on paper tickets by chalking the departure time on the wheels.

*Parked coaches in the permanently busy
tarmac close to Lake Windermere.*

*Photo stop by the Lake,
overlooking something of interest
in the life of Beatrix Potter.*

Parking up on the seafront awaiting the busload of pensioners to return from the fish and chip restaurant.

Welcome Aboard

LEFT THEN RIGHT

IN EMERGENCY ONLY TURN HANDLE

Some bus drivers improvised with the felt pen when the technology was not high end.

A familiar scene of wet cour roads from the front of the l

CHAPTER 6

GAN ON, YER POSH GIT

Discarding thirty-eight years of bachelorhood, when I moved into my wife's nineteenth century fisherman's cottage in a busy coastal town might have been a hard pill to swallow for someone so stuck in his ways. But it wasn't. It was the best thing that happened in my life. Newly married life was bliss. Of course, that's what every newlywed says, but I felt that I had been given an injection of purpose. Living in Whitley Bay was a novelty. It was an eclectic place, beautiful in parts with long sandy beaches, a church which resembled a mini-cathedral in Cullercoats and the rugged coastline around St Mary's Lighthouse. The centre was dominated by a white Moorish inspired building with an enormous dome, which was the tired and neglected local amusement park called the Spanish City. Many eclectically famous people hailed from Whitley Bay further adding to its bohemian image, including W.E. Johns, who wrote the Biggles books, the actor Robson Green, the artist John Gilroy and Gladstone Adams, the inventor of the windscreen wiper.

Though parts of Whitley Bay still retained their character, it was generally a grubby place.

It was once the most popular seaside resort in the North East. Gradually the fine Victorian buildings at nearby Tynemouth, such as the Piazza, were pulled down and the outdoor sea water swimming pool was closed and filled with rocks. The road which hugged the coastline suffered from the increased amount of traffic as the town became more reliant on being a dormitory town for Newcastle. There was a misconceived idea to turn the place into a shopping paradise and centre for nightclubs. Much to the local residents' consternation, the boisterous nightlife attracted a plethora of stag and hen parties. This led to Whitley Bay becoming scruffy and the pavements were strewn with litter, cigarette butts and the tell-tale white marks where chewing gum had been removed. The underpass to the beach had the strong whiff of ammonia and was a place where needles and syringes were discarded. There were brown streaks on many pavements where people had failed to avoid the piles of dog poop. On the beachfront, the old sign had been overlaid with many graffiti messages but it was still possible to just make out the faint writing underneath: WELCOME TO WHITLEY BAY

There were faint glimmers of a glorious past in the form of Scot's Week. Traditionally when the Scottish factories closed in July many Scots would come to Whitley Bay for their holidays. I would meet the odd few Glaswegians, walking on the sea front who said that they still observed the ritual of Glasgow Fair.

Even with the typical decline of many of Britain's seaside towns Whitley Bay refused to die. To the contrary, it was a thriving place and was the thirty-seventh most populated seaside town in Britain. The people were friendly and though many of the shops seemed to be house clearance specialists, junk shops and antique dealers, some old habits kept going. Every Friday afternoon a door-to-door seller sold styrofoam cups filled with white crabmeat, caught fresh and dressed that day for £1.

My wife's terraced cottage was in a pedestrian street with a communal garden in front of the house, making it feel like a leafy square. It was the perfect neighbourhood watch. Everybody therefore knew everyone else's business. Someone was always passing.

"Have you heard the shooting today, down the road, in the next door street?" asked a neighbour, slightly destroying the illusion of peace and happiness. "It's something to do with the Irish."

Chapter 6

The grapevine was robust in Whitley Bay and though we minded our own business, for some reason everyone told me things which were going on in the area. I had to stop leaning on the garden fence as it was an invitation for some passing gossip.

There was a large apple tree at the front of the house and when passersby saw me picking the fruit, putting them into an apple press and squeezing the juice, it did not take them long to figure out that there was a high probability of a free drink soon.

"Aye. We knew," said a neighbour. "We knew as soon as we heard the bangs coming from your house. That could only have meant one thing – that the bottles were exploding. And that meant that you must have made some cider."

The apple press had come from the next door street where there happened to be a home brew and winemaking business, run by an enterprising New Zealander who managed to make wine and sell it at £2-something a bottle. He found a way out of bypassing import duty by importing grape juice from his own vineyard in Bordeaux and making the wine in his shop, whereby VAT was the only applicable tax.

It was on one morning, quite possibly a cider-induced hangover of a morning, that I took the bull by the horns and searched for a closer bus company where I could get a job. I looked in the local papers and spotted a firm looking for drivers who were based within half an hour's drive from home, in an industrial town. They were based on an industrial estate on the outskirts of the town. The drive to the depot passed a stately home, a redundant harbour used mainly for loading coal, a sandy beach and a well known factory shop, with crowds of Japanese tourists milling around the entrance. The depot was close to a stretch of land where travellers regularly camped, despite the council's best preventative measures of placing concrete blocks on every grass verge and road entrance. There was also a helipad and a helicopter landed as I pulled into the car park. It appeared to skim the tops of the rows of parked buses. The vehicles shuddered and swayed in the down draft which belied their true age. At first sight, the depot had a ring of a bus graveyard more than a thriving bus company. My first impressions were therefore mixed. On a positive note the helicopter pilot must have been aided by the bus company as the waning sun shone on the oil and diesel slicked puddles, making them reflect so brightly that they could have been mistaken for landing lights.

On the other side of the depot there was a dark river. It was not an attractive river, particularly when the tide was out and the black mud banks took on the same viscous quality as the puddles in the depot. It was a cold spot being so close to its mouth and the sea and a ferocious, pesky wind blew and bit through the many layers of clothing I was wearing. But it was a curiously serene and tranquil spot. The peace would only be broken by occasional passing police cars with blaring sirens and council vans rushing to chase the local travellers who had yet again found a way round the boulders and camped on the grassy verge.

The various arrays of elderly buses seemed to deposit small quantities of oil wherever they were parked. Many had rust marks, presumably because of being kept out in the open and were prone to the sea salt from the constant wind. The security looked to be adequate, as the depot was surrounded by a chain link fence and there were cameras at selected points. I could hardly imagine anyone wanting to steal one of the buses. The second-hand value would hardly be worth the risk.

With that I walked into the non descript brick single storey building and met the owners. As in most bus companies I had visited in the past, there were two owners, a tall and thin one and a rotund one. These men had began life as ordinary bus drivers before deciding to branch out on their own. They had set up in a tough environment, discovering a niche and in knowing exactly what their customers wanted, they seemed to be thriving. In their town, that meant the cheapest price possible, a no frills service and plenty of humour. They sensibly rarely, if ever splashed out on new, expensive buses and preferred the older models, thereby owning them outright and not being beholden to the finance companies. Many a foolish bus company owner, I have seen, splashing out hundreds of thousands on a brand new bus and going bust within a year, because the North Eastern market was not that sort of place.

When I first walked into the main office to ask if there were any driver's vacancies, I encountered the sort of reaction I had become used to. I received some strange looks and pointed questions, before the desperation over the drought of drivers took precedence over targeted selectiveness. After I had been driving there for some time one of them said, "We thought bloody hell, what is this. You came in here with your posh accent and we thought you must be well and truly taking the piss."

They agreed to take me on. I was given a short introduction, before they announced,

"You're starting tomorrow morning, the Northern Terrier school run." I found out the next day that the Northern Terrier was a pub in an area which was the first pick-up point for some fiery school-children.

The area had suffered over the past two decades, losing its mining industry. The shipping was also severely cut back, the Miner's Strike had weakened the morale and there was high unemployment. My first challenge was to understand what the local people were talking about. The Northumbrian Pitmatic dialect was still much in evidence and took time to master. It was similar in one respect, yet very different from the Geordie I was used to. It was harsher in some ways, more poetic and lyrical in others.

"I'm going to go to the bingo tonight," one of the drivers announced at the end of a shift. I thought he said, "Ahm goer-in t'goeur t' da bin-goeur tonicht." It was a long process and stretched the patience of the other drivers as I asked them to repeat what they said for the eighth time.

My first morning at the depot was not easy.

It should have been a simple 30-minute drive from home to work, but that morning there was a sea fret along the coast road. Sea frets were common in that part of the world and tended to last for hours if not days. When the rest of the country was baking, disgruntled voices of fury could be heard all along the Northumbrian beaches. I arrived at the depot, flustered and late. I walked into the drivers' room, where all the jolly banter and jokes ceased immediately when I entered and were replaced with silence and deep suspicion. I could feel the icy stares examining my every move.

"Who the f**k is he?" I heard one driver say, as I walked out of the drivers' room and down the corridor towards the buses.

"Has management sent a spy?" said another.

"Bloody funny sort of spy," continued another. "He's a big'un, with a big nose. Funny, posh way of talking, too. He's not from round here."

I was handed my job sheet with the school run details on it. I hadn't a clue where I was supposed to go. It had been altered. I was no longer going to the Northern Terrier, but to a place I had never heard of. So I asked the nearest driver I saw. He was half my size and sported a firm, disdainful and serious look, as I disturbed him eating his breakfast.

"Excuse me, but can you tell me please how I get to Stakeford (it sounded more like 'Stakefud' in my southern accent)?"

He raised himself out of the chair, sighing as he put down his

Chapter 6

bacon sandwich and newspaper. He stood facing me, but only inches away and bent his neck upwards, giving me a hard stare. For the briefest moment I was worried. I thought he was winding himself up to hit me, but instead he firmly said, "It's Stake-FORD, STAKE-FOOORRRD, you posh git."

With that he marched off and started up his bus. This was the start of a good friendship and I enjoyed wholeheartedly going on trips with Lenny later on. They were never dull. Of course, this was once I had mastered his accent and comprehended that a 'mou-er' was a moor, anything sounding like 'herp' was hope and that the suburb of South Shields called Chichester is pronounced Chy-Chester and shortened to simply Chy. It is all very confusing.

Lenny owned a Fish and Chip shop in Ashington and drove buses in between frying up times. He had a friend who went fishing and once gave him some fresh halibut he had caught. Lenny battered them, fried them up and placed them in the warming cabinet. All the regular customers came in and one by one, they pointed at the fried halibut and said, "What's that, then?"

"Well that's a beautiful fish called halibut," replied Lennie.

" I'm not having that. I only like cod."

The only way he could sell it was to tell a white lie to his customers and say that the fish was a new variety of cod. The next day all the people who had taken the halibut came back into the shop to tell Lenny that it was the best fish that they had ever tasted and that this new variety of cod was something special.

Many of the bus drivers seemed to like fishing. One used to risk death by climbing over the outlet pipes from the local power station, as the water their was warm and the sea bass would congregate there. My early jobs with the bus company were all school runs. It involved going to some poor performing schools and transporting some earthy and sometimes lawless schoolchildren. The only law which they discussed on the bus was how they were going to sue their teachers.

"Tom. A piece of advice," a driver gave me in an early lesson on staying out of trouble. "Never admit liability – even if it is your fault. The big companies never do. Do as I did when I clobbered some car and just say the bus did it."

This seemed to be the general outlook on life in that part of the world. There was an ongoing scam for the replacement of low emission light bulbs. The inspector would walk into the house on an estate, count the number of lamps and write out a cheque supposedly to be used for buying some new fangled light bulbs. As the inspector bade farewell and went out the front door, there was a flurry of activity and the lamps were unplugged, taken out of the back door and bundled on to a waiting van. They were already in place at the next house, when the inspector rang the doorbell. This lamp carousel proved very lucrative and no one ever seemed to cotton on to the fact that the EU was paying 100 times too much for each light bulb.

The schools were quite unlike any I had been to before.

"Don't take me to that horrible town," screamed a hysterical schoolgirl, "they sell vast quantities of drugs there." The particular town was well known as being one of the most troublesome places. It was a grey and nondescript place. It was the sort of place where you only stopped if you urgently needed the public conveniences, and even then I would cross my legs and wait.

With the alleged proliferation of drugs, the schools were sometimes easy targets and there were occasionally sellers standing outside the school gates at 3.30 waiting to do business. I watched suspicious looking huddles from my bus. When the police came, they would move 300 yards further down the street and continue their trade. It had the air of somewhere which could erupt into violence at anytime.

One afternoon whilst I was waiting outside a school, a twenty-something thug, wearing a black leather jacket with a thick bald head, marched on to the bus and found the teenage schoolboy he was looking for. He pulled him off his seat and frogmarched him off the bus. Once he had got him on the pavement, he beat the living daylights out of him, before running off. Passers-by stood and watched. Some schoolgirls screamed. Nobody did anything to stop him (including myself). They all seemed to know the reason for this. It transpired that it was because the boy had just broken up with his girlfriend who was also at the same school, and that he was in debt to her. He owed her £5. She was so incensed about this, that she hired a goon to teach the boy a lesson, which must have cost her much more than a £5 note. It confirmed the phrase 'heaven has no rage like love to hatred turned. Nor hell a fury like a woman scorned,' as William Congreve wrote in *The Mourning Bride*.

Some of the younger children could also be spasmodically odious. When they were not thinking up scams to sue their teachers, they were letting off stink bombs, filling condoms full of water and viler substances and occasionally setting fire to the back seats, although they nearly always put the fires out. This was out of self-preservation and not just out of the goodness of their hearts. Usually some kind of mischief would happen on the way back to the Northern Terrier drop off point.

They rarely minced words and no one was safe from their observations. One little girl was the ringleader and made acerbic comments on most races, creeds and about most things in life. The others ignored her and used to say, "That's just Kayleigh. Don't listen to her, she's crackers. She changes boyfriends more than she changes her knickers."

The morning school run left the bus in a stinky and steamy state with rude messages which had been written with index fingers through the accumulated condensation on the windows. Some would board the bus with the lingering smell of deep fat frying attached to them. It was worsened when after shave, perfume, salt and vinegar crisps and sweet and fruity chewing gum were added to the equation.

I soon found out that my nose was a more resilient organ than I had previously thought and after a few days of driving the school bus, I was so used to the stench that I barely noticed it.

Other drivers found it harder. One, having pulled away from the school, saw two boys light up cigarettes as they sat down in their seats. From experience he knew that by confronting them, it would rile them and they would either take no notice or turn aggressive and violent. So instead at the next bus stop he stopped the bus, walked down the aisle and sat down in the adjacent seat and without saying a word. He then lit up a cigarette of his own and slowly smoked it. This unnerved the boys who had been removed from their comfort zone with the bus driver behaving in such an unusual way and they quickly stubbed their cigarettes out without saying a word. The driver returned to his seat and continue on his way.

The older children became even more of a handful. A few miles north of the town, there was a redundant mining village where one of the school runs started. To get to it the bus had to pass another foul stink caused by the emissions of a penicillin factory, which even caused the children to pinch their noses. I used to try and put the foot down, but as it was on a dual carriageway and the bus was at full permissible speed, it was never possible. When I got there the bus was swarmed with children fighting to get on the bus. They were segregated on the double-decker buses, with girls sent up to the top deck and the boys downstairs. Their school had a reputation as a place where persistent bullying took place. As I drove into the parking bays there were frequently fights between the boys. The girls loitered in menacing looking groups and looked on. Sometimes there would be a cat fight and two girls with dishevelled hair, ripped clothing, scratch marks and bruises on their cheeks would be pulled apart, still kicking and screaming, by the teachers. I drove the double-decker away as fast as I could.

On some of the school runs an elderly man called Landon sat in the front seat and acted as courier. He seemed to have a magical touch and was on the same wavelength as the children. The children worshipped him for his good-nature and down-to-earth humour. He knew all the children's names, their families, what trouble they were in, their likes and dislikes. He had a pet saying for each and every one.

But he could also be tough and hurled humorous put downs, such as: "Your hair is like wire, BARBED WIRE ... and your ears are like saucers – FLYING SAUCERS."

To the bus drivers he would offer advice and acted as amateur life coach. "You've gotta laugh now, as you won't when you are dead!"

He had a longstanding run in with one precocious boy with a haircut which was popular at the time and modelled on a David Beckham No. 2 style.

"I wish you were on the radio – then I would turn you OFF," he told him and "I've got my good shoes on, so I'm not going to give you a kick up the pants, as I will scuff the polish."

"Always remember this about this area – you go to this town laughing and you come back in stitches," he often reminded me. He was right. The town was a hard place. The bitter north easterlies whistle in off the North Sea into the middle of the modernised 1960's concrete town centre, made even the hardiest complain. Not that it deterred the weekend partygoers who wandered the streets wearing very little. The men were in t-shirts and shorts, the women in tank tops and miniskirts.

"I'd never had shoes, until it was that I went to the swimming baths one day – I stole them from the locker."

"Aye," said Landon, "we're tough. The Scots say 'all fur coat but no knickers'. But the reality is that no one can afford the fur coats here."

* * * * *

At the weekends I used to have to be prepared to do a late shift on Friday and Saturday nights. This was always bitter sweet, because no one likes giving up their weekends, but at the same stroke, the sights I saw made it worth every minute. The people of the town of Blyth had a passion at the weekends for travelling down to Whitley Bay and piling into the bars and nightclubs. Traditionally, Friday nights were reserved for boys' night out, Saturdays were for the ladies and Sundays were for couples, when they were on their best behaviour.

The bus company had spotted an opportunity and hit on a winning formula by running a once down, once back service. The trip to the Hairy Lemon nightclub in the heart of Whitley Bay cost £1-50 each way. Two double-deckers and some additional coaches were always full, with standing room only. The passengers were drunk before they boarded the buses but the downward journey was over quickly as the passengers were all in a good mood.

The return journey was a different matter altogether. I would park near the Hairy Lemon just before 11pm and wait for the bus to fill. The place was pandemonium. Hundreds of drunks spilled out of the clubs and bars on to the pavement. Several vanloads of police were always on duty, lined up on the opposite side of the street on the sea front. The policemen were twitchy, looking around apprehensively, as if they felt trouble was imminent. Experience must have told them that there was often a high percentage chance. When the punch-ups started in earnest, bottles flew through the air and disorder followed with people running in all directions, being pursued by policemen. The noise of the brawl would reach a high pitched crescendo with roars of encouragement from gangs of women (reading this now I find I ask myself what all the fuss is about, but back around the Millennium the drinking problems found in town and city centres were just beginning to get out of control.)

The tense atmosphere continued on to the return trip. Both sexes tried to jump into the driver's cab and cover the driver with slobbering kisses. Nine times out of ten, they would be so drunk that they would fall flat on their faces at the first hurdle, the front step. If they did manage to negotiate that hazard, the dribbling signs of drunken friendship were exhibited in their haste to kiss the driver. The plastic protective grill took the full brunt and a mixture of greasy finger marks and saliva would run down the plastic and dry in long smears. It took an extra half an hour to clean the bus on returning to the depot, even longer than after a school run.

The girls were usually were the worst. They packed a powerful punch as they wanted to fight everyone they saw. Even the most beautiful, innocent looking, petite blonde or brunette was a potential danger. Their eyes flashed wildly and were smudged with running mascara. They could produce an upper cut or right hook of such quality, that the recipient male would be knocked out on the floor of the bus. Usually this was accompanied by cheers and then the sound of a stampede of policemen in their hobnailed boots boarding the bus.

There was a particularly unpleasant argument between a group of friends who fell out over something trivial and it quickly descended into a brawl. Their punches rarely connected as when they swung their fists, they would overbalance and their legs would give way. There was a medieval etiquette to the fight. They would take it in turns to hit each other. Girl would hit boy. Boy would hit other girl. Girl would then wallop girl. Boy would strike boy and returned the compliment. When they had all had a go, the process would begin again.

The double-decker would sway from side to side because of the fighting on the top deck. The rest of the passengers would sit and stare out of the windows into the blackness or fall asleep.

The police were good at handling most dramas in Whitley Bay. They dealt with minor incidents with a surprising amount of patience and sense of fun. A policeman came on to my bus when he noticed that three overweight girls were misbehaving.

"They were flashing their tits and arses at me out of the window," he said, "we can't be having that." The girls came down the stairs to meet him, quickly lowered their tank tops, pouted provocatively and propositioned him by saying: "Do you want us then, pet?"

"Certainly not," replied the constable. "You are too spotty." The girls adjusted their boob tubes and sat down again, visibly deflated. They never said another word all the way back home.

There were, however, worse places than the nightclub region in Whitley Bay where I had to drive to. One private hire involved taking a party for a night to the dog racing. Greyhound racing has never been known as a violent sport; I used to race greyhounds myself and never saw any bad behaviour.

Close to this particular track was a nightclub, where the punters retired to, after racing finished. The last race was usually around 10pm, but they did not emerge until the early hours of the morning.

As I sat in the freezing car park, two men came out of the nightclub. One had a knife and exploded when he saw another man who also gripped a knife leaning against the opposite side of the chain link fence which separated the club from the car park. It was the first time I had ever seen two men with knives try and stab each other through a fence. They were so impatient to attack each other that neither could be bothered to walk a few yards through the gate. The fence made the fight ineffectual and after a few minutes both men realised that it was a waste of energy and neither men could get their blades anywhere near the other.

Then a bizarre thing happened. They returned their knives to their pockets, smiled at each other, met in the gateway and shook hands.

Shortly afterwards, the first waves of women came out. The first wave were tipsy and clutching their knees together, desperately wanting a pee. They made a zigzag manoeuvre for the nearest bushes. The second wave of women, who came out of the club were paralytic. Some fell horizontally on to the hard ground, when they came into contact with the night air and were out cold. They were then dragged by the legs, by their men folk, like wheelbarrows, with their heads bumping along behind on the gravel. The group who had hired the bus did not appear until 2am, having said they would be no later than 1 o'clock. They were in a similar condition and were so far gone that they were speechless and had little or no control of most of their bodily functions. I had to drag them on to the bus. When we arrived at their destinations, they were comatose and I had to remove them one by one. At the end, I was exhausted and fed up. They didn't give any tip. They could not find their pockets, though every cloud has a silver lining and when I cleaned the bus there were a large number of coins lying under the seat, which must have fallen out of their pockets. It amounted to something which was more than if they had actually given a tip.

The bus company had a habit of taking on jobs which few other organisations would touch. Take the Sunderland football supporters.

Many times I ventured into the depths of Sunderland and picked up football fans, driving them all across the country to the away matches. One of the reasons the supporters liked us, besides being cheap, was because there was a relaxed attitude to what they could drink on the bus.

The coaching industry, in the main, had complied with a voluntary code of practice when it came to transporting football fans to a match, meeting certain guidelines set by the police. Under the terms of Section 1 (1) of the Sporting Events (Control Of Alcohol) Act 1985 as amended by the Public Order Act 1986, the carriage of alcohol was prohibited on a Passenger Service Vehicle taking passengers to or from a designated sporting event. The supporters we carried drank wholesomely. Cans of lager were sunk at a speedy rate a for three quarters of any trip. Even though the regulations were only just beginning to be enforced, driving a busload of drunken football fans was a risky business.

"What are you worried about, mate?" my co-driver said, detecting my obvious unease. "I've been doing this job for years and I know exactly how it works." I bit my tongue, but it failed to improve the feeling of nervousness I had the whole trip.

A flurry of activity would occur on the bus, usually twenty miles or so from the ground, where the hurried bundling up of any evidence into black bin liners would be followed by a stop in some lay by and the contents dumped in a bin. This complied with the law, in so far as coaches were not allowed to stop within ten miles of a venue, either on the way in or out, but flaunted it in other ways. The bus then continued on to the football ground and the supporters looked quite angelic as they came down the steps.

It all nearly came to grief once when the bus had a puncture and a load of men in red and white striped football shirts rampaged through a pub car park less than an hour's drive from the ground as the wheel was fixed. It would have been a big problem if the police had arrived as there had not been time to clear the bus and the Black Cats fans were displaying all the early signs of drunkenness.

Several of the trips to the football grounds were exciting affairs. It was run like a military operation and the police required all buses to drive along a specific route and park well away from any home supporters. On the return journey from the match the away buses were given a police escort and drivers were asked to drive at speed through the city. Liverpool was notoriously bad and we were stoned by the local youths at three or four street corners. There were cracks on some of the windows but none broke. Coventry too was volatile and I watched the bus in front of me have its rear window smashed to smithereens. Following closely I just put my foot down and good fortune helped us run the gauntlet and we survived the hail of rocks and other missiles which rattled on the bus roof.

In addition to the football matches, I was subjected once more to yet more antics of a rugby club tour. This time it was a friendly club. They were by no means a rich club, but they travelled the length and breadth of the country playing much wealthier clubs in their league. They were soundly beaten by a club in Cheshire, 49-0. But to put things into perspective, the Chester players were semi-professional and said they received a £100 fee each match, whereas our lowly club players had to pay to play and coughed up a £2.50 sub each time they played.

They made up for it after the match by drinking solidly for four hours, before boarding the bus. On the way back they stopped off for a night out in Lancaster. They behaved as all rugby clubs seem to behave post match. I was used to this, having just returned from a trip to the continent where a rugby club had ran riot on the ferry returning home. Half an hour out of port they had monopolised the bar; 45 minutes out, they were well on the way to drinking the ship dry and singing bawdy songs and after an hour they were rampaging round the ship, causing havoc everywhere they went. The ship's staff hid meekly in the broom cupboard, leaving all the passengers to the mercy of the hordes.

Though this club went on a tempestuous spree in Lancaster city centre and drank the pubs dry, they collapsed back on to the bus at 1 am and went to sleep. I counted myself lucky.

* * * * *

My time at the seaside bus company ended when I had a chance to return to the Northumbrian countryside with my wife and new baby. It had been a great experience and I had learnt much from the bus company by the sea. They were a friendly lot. Before I went, I was requested to drive a wedding party for a relative of one of the directors. The indignant bride who, whilst struggling in all her finery to mount the steep steps of the bus, turned to me and yelled:"Don't look! You're not going to get a free look up my hoops!"

I spoke to the owner of the bus company at the top of the hill again and explained that my bus driving days were over because my wife had a better job and therefore I was going to become a househusband and look after our new baby daughter, Violet.

"That's no excuse," the boss said. "That won't stop you driving. You can take her with you."

So I did.

Chapter 6

CHAPTER 7

TAKING BABY
ON THE BUS

Two little girls were standing nervously on the roadside verge, awaiting the school bus to take them to the local First School on the first day of the new term. They were my two daughters. They kept asking me, in increasing excitement, if the driver would be Alistair. As the bus drove over the hill it was possible to make out the immaculately dressed figure at the wheel, wearing a white shirt with epaulettes and an electric blue tie. It could only be Alistair, one of a dying breed of staunch and upright bus drivers of the old school. He was in his early seventies and though mainly bald, he would always slick back his remaining hair in precisely the same position. He was loved and respected by children, teachers and parents alike.

The bus came to a halt. The doors opened and the two girls clambered up the steps.

Rose, the youngest, aged four plucked up the courage and asked him, "What's your name?"

"It's ... Rumplestiltskin," replied Alistair in a deadpan voice. She was momentarily stunned, before giving a broad smile and going to find her seat. It was to set the tone for future years of travelling on the school bus where the ambience was so warm and friendly. It was the perfect start to school life and possibly something she will never forget.

In rural North of England the school bus was a big part of a child's life. As the distances between home and school were so large, many children spent up to two hours each day on the school bus from an early age. A school bus driver was an influential figure. There were some loved characters like Alistair . There were many more grumpy school bus drivers who came into conflict with either the children, the parents or both.

Some drivers used to shout at the children, which resulted in even worse behaviour from the children. One incident ended up in court, when a driver, while driving through a city centre was being hit over the head with a safety hammer (for breaking the glass) as he drove. He slammed on the brakes at a busy junction, got up and chased the boy down the bus with the fire extinguisher. Another driver became so fed up with his schoolchildren that he stopped in the middle of the road, turned off the engine and walked away from the bus, leaving everyone stranded. The traffic soon mounted up until another driver could be found.

The providers of school buses were a mixed bunch. One bus company tried to cut corners by having two of their buses meet in a remote country spot, where they transferred the children off one bus on to the other, thereby saving diesel. But they got caught. Some school buses should not have been on the road. One looked like a converted bread van. Another didn't have seats, meaning that children had to sit on the floor in the aisle, using their school bags as cushions. Some had spongy wheels, some leaked, some were so rusty that it was possible to see right through from one side to the other. Some had moss growing in the inside. Parents and relatives rarely complained. They must have realised that their children were at the bottom of the pile when it came to spending money on buses. I don't think they cared, so long as the vehicle got them to school, belching black, white or yellow smoke.

My older daughter, Violet, was subjected to buses from babyhood. Early on she met Myrtle, the long established purple council playbus which toured Northern England. One of its remits, when

Myrtle was set up, was to combat social exclusion and stop parents and children living in the more isolated spots in the county from being cut off. Purple Myrtle Mark II followed. It was a brand new converted bus whose facilities were basically a slimmed down nursery or playgroup. The children would sit on the floor of the top deck and listen to stories, while downstairs there were tables for drawing and making things.

Times changed and a combination of rising costs, changing demographics and aspirations meant there was less need for Purple Myrtle, so it was decided to sell her off. My daughter cried as she saw it for the last time on ebay.

My wife had a full-time job and returned to work after maternity leave. I thereafter started taking on the challenge of juggling the mundane life of looking after a baby with driving buses. I decided to take my six month old daughter on the bus with me, looking after her during the day, in between shifts. It was on a suck it and see basis and I had my doubts as to whether it would be manageable.

Surprisingly, I managed well, provided it was run like a military operation.

I was up at 5.30am. It was dark and frosty as it was autumn turning to winter. I got a grumpy baby up, fed, dressed, nappy changed and raced to put the car seat and baby into the car, for the 15-minute drive to the depot. I usually arrived at the depot at 6.30am, left the baby in the car with the engine running and heater on, fought with the temperamental locks on the main door, turned the lights on, found out which bus I was driving to Newcastle that day, checked the oil and water, started the engine and turned the heating up high.

Then I ran back out to the car, took the baby in the car seat and strapped her into the front seat of the bus. I rushed back and forth between the car and the bus carrying full bottles, nappies, baby wipes, bottles of orange yoghurt dessert as well as destination board, waybill, Almex mechanical ticket machine and tachographs. Finally it was a race to fill in all the details needed to start the trip, do a walk round the bus checking lights, wheel nuts etc, checking all baby problems and finally opening the rollerdoors so that the bus left the depot on time at 6.55am and picked up the first passenger who was standing outside the depot, examining her watch.

The first time I did this it was chaotic. I had no idea what I was doing. After the initial pandemonium, it became easier and I developed a subconscious system where I seemed to run on autopilot. It ran so smoothly that I became blasé about the whole procedure. On one particular morning, when I had just finished all checks, it all went horribly wrong. Violet was ensconced on the bus and seemed to be mischievously happy, throwing her bottle of warm milk down at every opportunity and splattering the newly mopped floor. At the last moment I remembered that I had left something in the car and rushed out the side door to get it.

As I ran out of the depot, a gust of wind blew the door shut and I heard the Yale lock click into place. I turned around to my horror to see that there was no key on in the lock. The keys were lying on the bus seat next to Violet. As she was fascinated with all things glittery which jangled, I had left them for her to play with. In my haste I had also forgotten to raise the shutter doors, meaning that the depot was totally secure and there was no other way of getting in.

I felt sick. What was I going to do?

I progressed from feeling ill to the beginnings of a blind panic. Here was a situation where there was a baby on a cold bus with its engine running, blowing out exhaust fumes, locked inside a cold depot with no chance of being able to get in. It was dark and raining heavily. It was 6.30 in the morning. You could hear a pin drop as little stirred in, except for the gently purring sound of the engine ticking over. It turned colder as the rain turned to snow. An unthinkable nightmare.

I strode up and down with my feet making prints in the newly covered snow, and thought what I was going to tell my wife. My inner voice tried to control my jellified legs and arms by repeating over and over again, "Don't panic. Don't panic." But it was no help.

As the inner workings of my brain began to whirr into action, I remembered that one of the drivers lived relatively close and that he might have a spare key. I ran off in search of him. After a few false starts of knocking on the wrong door and receiving angry stares, I found him. Godfrey came down the stairs slowly. His bloodshot eyes betrayed the fact that he had obviously been on the beer the night before and it took time for him to become aware of the stupid thing I had done. He laughed and reached for his spare set of keys.

We sprinted to the depot and hurriedly opened the door. I was expecting the worst. It had been twenty minutes since the door had slammed shut. We were greeted with a different sight. There was Violet, happy as a lark, gurgling merrily and jangling the bunch of keys, occasionally trying to chew one. She was quite unperturbed by her missing father or the diesel fumes which were swirling around the depot. She had no idea she had been locked in. I needn't have worried.

The first time I took her to Newcastle, it proved to be a difficult trip. Violet was strapped into the seat behind me. The passengers were highly suspicious and disapproving of their bus driver taking his baby with him. Not least for the fact that she occupied one of the prime seats on the bus which was always popular as it had the best view and was easy to get in and out of. The front of the bus was where the commuter club gathered and was usually very social with lively banter about the local gossip. I could feel the angst amongst them as their routine was disrupted.

It came to a head one morning when Violet was in a vile mood and started to cry persistently, aggravated by the fact that she was hungry. I stood up and thought the only way forward was to be brutally honest with the passengers.

"I am afraid that Violet needs feeding," I said, "the choice is yours, either I can stop the bus, feed her and we will arrive in Newcastle fifteen minutes late, or one of you can come and sit beside her and feed her and we will be there on time."

There was silence.

Then a queue of people formed up at the front of the bus and volunteered to help. It seemed to break the ice and from that moment on Violet became a familiar face on the local bus scene. Everyone who came on the bus would talk to her, or smile and say "Hello Violet pet". She had an enormous amount of attention and the passengers fed her bottles at any time. They also tried their best to temper their language replacing shit with sugar and more. The odd words which slipped out were invariably picked up by Violet and repeated later.

Once as I drove her to a playgroup, she was in her car seat on the back seat of a car this time, without warning said, "Oh my God."

"Violet you can't say that," I prudishly reprimanded her. "Say something like oh my goodness."

"Oh OK," she muttered then she fell silent for what seemed a long time. After a couple of minutes, she said,

"I suppose that means I can't say bugger either?"

Chapter 7

On the road, many people seemed to notice the bus driver and his baby. I have no idea why, because the sight of a baby in a baby seat strapped into the seat directly behind the driver, passers-by assumed that it could only mean one thing, that it must be his baby. Several motorists and pedestrians gaped with open mouths. Violet in a Polish grey hat in the shape of a mouse which complemented her yellow romper suit and red shoes had the effect of making other motorists lose their concentration and have to brake hard. Two taxis nearly collided. Pedestrians were similarly transfixed and I saw a woman walk into a lamppost while her head was turned, looking up at the bus window.

Having dropped off the passengers at the central bus station, at 9 o'clock, the day was free until it was time to pick up the passengers on the return journey at 5.00pm. We would either go to the bus company depot on the outskirts of the city, where Violet would spend the day watching me cleaning buses or sitting in a dark and dingy office with the other drivers.

"You don't want to bring a baby here," said a driver in a most concerned voice. "It's like a pig pen." He was right as the place stank of engine oil and grease and dry rot. But it was a lively depot, shared with another bus company and there was always something going on. It was a very sociable start for any baby. Violet was surrounded by bus drivers covered in dust and oil, who were gentle and kind, heaping attention on to her. Sometimes she came home with grease marks on her cheeks.

If I drove the college bus to a different city, the day was more varied. Having dropped off all the passengers, we would then stop at a sandwich shop and order a Cumberland sausage baguette for me and a bacon sandwich for Violet which we would munch in the coach park. The rest of the day would be spent wheeling the pushchair all over the city, through shops, museums, soft play centres, the park, the playground and beside the river where we would have picnics.

In the afternoon she would fall asleep on the bus. Those were idyllic days when the sun shone, but when it rained or snowed we just sat on the bus. It did not matter, because we played until she was tired and went off to sleep. The time flew by and it felt like a privilege for me to get to know my daughter so well.

I became proficient at nappy changing on the go, learning where all the baby friendly places were. The bus was a godsend. It was our refuge. For changing nappies, it was a luxury. There were fifty-three seats to choose from, ignoring the driver's seat. So many Dads would come back from work and have a few minutes with their child and here I was being able to be with my daughter for the whole day.

Having a baby on the bus helped even when you were subjected to a flying visit from the Vehicle Inspectorate (renamed VOSA these days). One evening in the city coach park, a plain white Ford parked itself beside the buses and before I knew it a man leapt up at the windscreen, brandishing an identity card.

"Open the door," he impatiently asserted. "Spot check."

I never messed with the Vehicle Inspectorate as they had a clear agenda to stick to and wielded great power if anyone hindered their mission. I'm sure they realised the pressures bus companies and bus drivers were under and Sometimes she came home with grease marks on her cheeks. Every now and then I was examined by an overzealous bureaucrat who threw his weight around. I thought this was going to be one of those times.

The inspector strode up the steps and continued his menacing attitude. He looked as if he meant business and was going to be awkward and officious. As he was about to launch into his list of questions, he was momentarily distracted by Violet gurgling and being sick in her car seat. It completely put him off his stride.

Chapter 7

"What the blazes is that?" he said in a slightly kinder voice.

He sat down next to Violet, put his notebook away and launched into adult baby talk. For the next twenty minutes he asked me about potty training, teething problems and told me how he and his wife coped with sleepless nights with their baby. Then he returned to official mode and checked my tachographs and the roadworthiness of the bus.

I have seen the same inspector since at other checks around the county. He always remembered me and asked how the baby was.

It is unusual to find a boss who took such a relaxed attitude to things such as babies on buses, but he actively encouraged my babysitting duties while driving his buses. I would never have considered it on my own. When my wife was able to look after Violet more, purely because she was expecting Rose, our second daughter, I drove without any babies in the back of the bus and I was surprised to find that I seemed to suffer something akin to withdrawal symptoms.

When Rose was born. I tried to do the same again, and in a manner of fashion, it worked, though a toddler and a baby was a different proposition. But Violet was getting to an age where she needed more. She needed to go to toddler groups, then nurseries and playgroups. Rose, on the other hand was at the age to visit breast feeding and baby groups.

I declined the breast feeding groups for the sake of decency, but I went to the many baby groups. Being the only man there, I was mother hen'd by the other mothers, who seemed to feel that I needed all the help I could get. I sat around, drinking cups of coffee and being force-fed biscuits and unsurprisingly I balooned.

The bus driving I did less and less. There just wasn't time to fit everything in. I still did the odd job, and the boss asked me to do a private hire taking a group to a local town and return late at night.

"It will be a long one," he said, "but I know them all and there won't be any trouble."

How wrong could he be?

Violet at the wheel, entertaining herself in the long wait in the coach park.

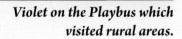

Violet on the Playbus which visited rural areas.

Feeling sleepy after a large lunch of sausages and strawberries.

Evidence of the constant battle between bus drivers and parking wardens.

CHAPTER 8
IT ENDED WITH
A STABBING

Taking parties from the local area was usually never any problem. In the unlikely event of something going wrong there was always some comeback, everybody knew everybody and if anybody misbehaved, their reputation was soiled in the local community. Transporting a full bus load to a town forty minutes away therefore should have been straightforward, even if it was to watch a football match, where there would be excessive all day drinking.

The town I was driving to, in its heyday was a thriving market town, surrounded by prosperous agriculture, coal mining, quarrying and a brickworks. Now it relied on tourism, arts, crafts and agriculture. It also had a reputation as a place which attracted aggravation and where fights were not unknown at the weekend. The fights on odd occasions had descended into full scale riots.

On that particular Sunday the local Tyne & Wear derby between Newcastle United and Sunderland was being broadcast live on Sky. The two cities, barely ten miles apart had their differences for centuries, from Newcastle being Royalist and Sunderland, Parlimentarian during the English Civil War. During the 1745 Rebellion, one was pro Hanoverian and the other supported Bonny Prince Charlie, so perhaps it was no surprise to see the rivallry extend to supporters at football matches. But the intense interest encompassed the whole North East and the working men's club in this town had a huge screen, and more importantly all beer was only £1 per pint. Armed with that knowledge the return journey was going to be lively but there was no expectation of trouble.

When I returned to pick them up at 10 o'clock that night, the atmosphere had changed and the town now had a menacing air. The streets were filled with boisterous, drunk men and women bristling for a fight. The town had security cameras at every corner, but there was a local joke that whenever there was an incident, they always mysteriously were pointing in the other direction.

The 10.30 departure time came and went. People trickled back to the bus in dribs and drabs, starting with the most sober. The later arrivals were very drunk and the stragglers were legless. Strangely I noticed that we seemed to have picked up some extra passengers, as there was not one spare seat and there had been several empty seats on the downward journey. But there was no cause for alarm as everyone seemed to know the new faces and the organisers were happy to give them a lift back home.

At first the journey back went smoothly enough with only a few of the usual bawdy but harmless football songs being sung in honour of the earlier 1-1 draw between the rival clubs, but without warning the bus started rocking violently from side to side. There was increased shouting and screaming which meant only one thing – a fight had broken out.

One of the people travelling was an off-duty bus driver. He staggered down the aisle and with slurred difficulty, tried to tell me that one of the passengers had walked from the front of the bus to the back, wagged his finger at some of the men in the back, uttered some insults, thereby starting the punch-up.

As he was telling me this, he managed to take his mobile phone out of his pocket and dial 999, handed me the phone and passed out. I was reluctant to talk to the police as I thought if I waited a bit the situation would calm down and we could drive on . We only had 3 miles to go.

But I had no choice as the operator answered quickly and told me to wait where I was because a police car was on the way, promising it would be long. That turned out to be an empty promise as we waited and waited for what seemed like an eternity. Forty minutes later the police still had not arrived. We heard their sirens and in the distance saw the blue lights going from the hilltops on one side of the valley, down to the valley floor and then on top of another hilltop on the opposite side, then back again. They were obviously lost.

The mood on the bus was turning increasingly ugly. The fight had long ceased and the protagonists , when they heard the police were on their way had leapt off the bus and decided to walk back to town. Their last words to me were: "We'll be back before you will be." Annoyingly they would be right.

I was left to wait for the police with a busload of drunk but slowly sobering up people, who were completely innocent and all they wanted to do was to get home. They were tired and fed up. The suppressed anger was mounting and the bus felt like a volcano waiting to erupt. Not only were they venting their spleens on me, but it felt like a second fight could break out at any moment. I preferred standing outside the bus in the cold air than having to listen to the poisonous mutterings.

As things looked at their direst, the police arrived. The ruddy faced policeman leapt out of his Volvo looking harassed, flushed and embarrassed.

"We couldn't find you, mate. They must have given us the wrong directions," the officer told the passengers. This poor explanation did not pacify the people on the bus. It made them angrier, but it took the heat off me as they directed snide remarks at the policeman and forced him off the bus.

"I've been driving so fast, I could fry an egg on the bonnet," said the driver of the second police car which rolled up. He looked anxiously at the steam rising from the beneath the bonnet.

"I know, we saw you exploring most of the Pennine hilltops individually," sneered one irate passenger. The policeman stiffened but did nothing.

A third squad car drove up, followed by a fourth. This must have meant that all the police's resources in a 50-mile radius had been deployed on this one incident on the bus, leaving many conurbations without cover. If only the criminals had realised. It would have been their benefit night.

I explained the circumstances to one of the policeman. He realised the situation was still explosive and could ignite at anytime, but when I asked him if he would mind coming on to the bus and reading the riot act, to my horror he replied, "No. I couldn't possibly do that, it might inflame the situation." Neither would he accede to the request to put his blue light on and follow the bus to its destination. This was for the fear of crossing the boundary from one county into another and the resulting consequences, problems and added paperwork it would undoubtedly bring.

My final try was to ask him to ring the local policeman in the town we were heading for and ask him to come out, but he said he would not wake him at this hour in the morning. So that was that, I was on my own.

I was nervous as I drove back and wondered what was going to happen now. I felt in my bones that it wasn't going to be something good. As the bus pulled up in the town centre, I spotted the men who had been fighting, who said they would get back before I did. They were happily standing outside the pub downing pints.

Half of the busload started to disembark and I watched them

stagger down the aisle in my mirror. One of the last passengers to get off was a younger girl who was the girlfriend of one of the fighters. As she passed a group of women, including the wife of the instigator of the fight, she was jumped on, forced on to the floor, then, viciously kicked, punched and bitten. It was the first time in my life that I had witnessed a catfight and it was not pleasant. Any hint of dignity and decorum vanished in a cloud of flailing arms and legs. It was over before anyone could prise them apart and the shaken girl picked herself up, ran down the steps and into the pub.

The main troublemaker joined his vicious wife and barked at me to drive back to the depot as fast as I could. They were laughing and obviously satisfied with proceedings. The fighting ladies rushed up to the front of the bus and, one by one gave me a hug and a kiss, in a 'nudge nudge, wink wink, say no more' manner. In a cowardly way I said nothing for the sake of not wanting to ignite anything over the last few miles we had to travel.

I dropped them off near the depot and felt relieved as I watched them heading off in the direction of the pub. But as I was filling up the bus with diesel, I heard a commotion from the other side of the road, followed by screams and shouts. I could take no more and shut the garage doors, before making a quick escape to my car and the sanctuary of my bed.

The next morning I heard what the commotion was about. The instigator of the fight had been stabbed by the boyfriend of the beaten up girl. The previous night when she had got off the bus and had gone to the pub, the boyfriend had been so enraged by her appearance that he had driven up to the village, ahead of the bus and had waited in the shadows behind a building with a knife. He had allegedly stabbed the man in the chest, missing his lung by an inch.

When the policeman came to interview me, he said it was all due to a grudge. The area was well known for family feuds which tended to surface every ten years or so, with a brief explosion of violence before returning to peaceful ways again. True to form, the person who was stabbed refused to press charges, even though he had been stabbed to within an inch of his life. The police took it seriously and did not like the prospect of people running around with knives in a tranquil rural area which was mainly problem free.

I gave a statement and the police said that they were going to pursue this case doggedly. The accused man was charged with grievous bodily harm with intent, was found guilty and served some time in prison.

The incident hastened my departure away from the world of buses. It seemed to be a convenient time to take a break. The birth of my second daughter, Rose, turned life upside down. My wife's salary against that of a bus driver was no competition, so it seemed better that I became a househusband for a second time.

Take two babies on the bus? It worked for a while, but I found that I needed more time off to transport the girls to various toddler and playgroups. The bus company were generous and offered me work more or less whenever I wished. I would return as soon as I could.

Little did I realise, that it would not be for a long time.

SEVEN
YEARS
LATER

Chapter 8

CHAPTER 9

WELCOME BACK: SNOW, YORKSHIRE BREAKFASTS, THE FLYING PIG AND TROUBLE IN THE LAND THAT GOD FORGOT

The first day back was a shock. After a seven-year break of nappy changing, chicken nugget cooking, washing clothes and dusting the house, it is easy to become detached from what's going on in the world. It was a strange sensation the first time at sat in the driver's seat. I instantly returned to making the same mistakes I had made when I was a newly qualified driver. The only difference seemed to be that I tended to make them in a calmer and less panicked way. In fact, after a few days I started to become overconfident as I felt I had seen it all before.

It was not helped by the fact that I had chosen the worst winter for eighteen years to return to driving. The snow began as light flurries but rapidly developed into blizzards. Unfortunately the more it snowed, the more it exposed my rustiness because of being away for so long and the worse my driving became. I made some bad mistakes.

In 2004, Frank Partridge wrote an article in *The Independent*, describing the hostile climate in the hills surrounding the depot. "Despite global warming," he warned, "snow does still fall in these parts, but is usually accompanied by weather of such ferocity that the inhabitants are strongly advised not to venture outside at all..."

It was at around 2000ft above sea level that I became bogged over the highest bus route in England. I thought of Mr Partridge as I sat alone, waiting for help to arrive. In the first two weeks I was back driving, I managed to get stuck in snowdrifts twice. There was a close shave, too, and a third accident was narrowly avoided when the bus slid on black ice.

"Well I've seen some stupid things in my time," snarled one of the bosses as he came to dig me out in the howling blizzard, "but this takes the biscuit." The second time he just shook his head and muttered: "What are you? A bloody disaster area – that's what you are," as he walked past, trying to wipe the gathering snow away from his face.

The first one happened on a notoriously bad bit of road which takes you over an alpine style ridge bordering two counties, commonly known as The Spade. No one knew precisely how it got its name, but the consensus was that it is due to countless hours spent in the past shovelling away the snow.

It was icy. I felt the bus slither slightly from side to side on the frozen road which should have been a caution not to attempt the exposed road over the high summit. The other drivers had not taken any chances, preferring to go around the long way. I foolishly went the fastest way to try to hurry back to the depot.

I also had fair warning on the journey down when I was tentatively inching down the hill smugly thinking how well I was doing until everything in the bus went ghostly quiet. All wheels lost their traction and the bus started heading sideways into the bridge wall and picking up speed rapidly. All I could do was to cling tightly on to the steering wheel and pray. Everything went into slow motion and once again my mind was filled with a multitude of extraordinary thoughts, not least of how I was going to explain to the boss that I had crashed his bus.

I had experienced that sort of feeling before in my life. There was the Australian bus crash (Chapter 1) and I once had a greater sense that I was about to die during a frightening landing at Beijing Airport in an ancient Russian Tupolev 154, which seemed to be coming in far too fast. I remember looking around at my fellow passengers, seeking their reaction, but they were only laughing and joking with each other. The aircraft hit the runway with a bang, shot up in the air again, nudged the tarmac with the wing tip, before bouncing three times and eventually shuddering to a halt at the end of the runway. Everyone clapped.

This time there was only me, so instead of clapping I just shut my eyes and waited for the collision. None came. Miraculously the bus corrected itself at the very last moment and slewed round the bend missing the bridge and the stone walls by millimetres. I sat for a while and shivered as the delayed shock kicked in and the realisation dawnedof how lucky I had been.

I was not the only one. Two other drivers had recently nearly lost a bus on the continent. Manic Martin and Fast Edwin were coming down a mountain road in the Austrian Alps late at night with a busload of schoolchildren on a skiing holiday. They skidded and hit a wall during their descent. The wall had done its job and had saved the bus from plummeting down hundreds of feet to the bottom of the mountain. The second time was inexcusable as I was trying to get back to the depot as quickly as possible totally disregarding the signs of heavy snowfalls. I was no different to the other drivers who loved to be the first back to the depot as it meant not having to queue for the pressure washer and diesel pumps. It meant getting home earlier.

The hilltop was covered in a blanket of fog and low cloud, which was not unusual due to its altitude. The other bus which was following me I noticed had stopped abruptly at the bottom of the hill, for no apparent reason. Perhaps the bus had broken down. Whatever the reason was, I was halfway up the hill, only five minutes away from the depot and in no mood for stopping.

I went round the sharp bend, accelerating to begin the slow climb and ascended into the cloud. Disastrously, it was not just a normal cloud but a snow cloud and it was blowing a blizzard. No wonder the other bus had stopped at the bottom. The driver had recognised the signs, turned round and had gone round the long way.

My ageing Volvo bus started to slow and slide in the deepening snow and came to a halt as it quickly lay five inches deep, part covering the wheels. I was scuppered. There was no way forward and no way back. The sharp bend behind me was now covered with snow, eliminating the chance of reversing. There was no mobile phone reception and the bus was being slowly buried under the blizzards and drifting snow.

This was a double disaster as I was due at my daughter Violet's 9th Birthday treat, a supper in the Chinese restaurant in a town eighteen miles away. Here I was stuck on the top of this miserable and desolate Northumbrian hilltop, unable to contact anybody.

The first sign of rescue came in the form of a lady in her small car, which came slewing up the hill with all wheels spinning and, against all odds, was making good progress. Without stopping, she leant over to the passenger seat, lowered the window and managed to shout a message out that she would get help if she made it over to the other side. She must have made it because the two bosses appeared in their car half an hour later, equipped with shovels. The snow was coming down fast in large flakes and horizontal.

We dug the bus out and I returned to the depot.

When I got back the word was out that some idiot had got his bus stuck in a snowdrift. For the next two weeks I had to suffer acerbic comments and the new nickname of Scott after Scott of the Antarctic, who was another, as the boss pointed out who always got stuck in the snow.

Mike the Mechanic put his head round the office door as I was receiving my dressing down. He looked displeased and stared daggers at me as he told the boss that the alternator was not charging anymore and that the likely cause of this was because I had kept all the lights on and the heaters at full blast while waiting to be rescued. It was all too much for the alternator.

After several days of heavy snowfalls, the village where the bus depot was took on a reluctant air of beauty. The three feet walls of snow and industrial sized icicles covered the usual slag heaps. The dour, grey landscape perked up a bit. The centre of the village for a short period seemed to resemble Lapland more than the normal Dodge City. All the snow had been pushed on to the pavements, the roads were narrow and the cars were parked in a horseshoe pattern around the pub. Everybody seemed to be in some sort of holiday mood in the extreme cold with temperatures down to –10 degrees Celsius.

However these winter wonderland picture postcard scenes were no good for buses or bus driving. It was always a difficult depot to get into and out of, due to its narrow entrance. Owing to the poor lighting there was a high probability of reversing into one of the metal pillars at the sides of the building, which I was prone to do even in dry conditions. The walls of snow made bus movements more restrictive and awkward. When the buses eventually made it out of the depot they did not like the snow and tended to skid around, especially the ones with automatic gearboxes.

The snow had not abated since my last disaster and a few days later I had another bad day. It had not started well from the moment I got out of bed. I knew the snowstorm during the night would make it very hard to get to the depot. It was a big ask for my Renault Laguna Estate, so another driver offered to give me a lift. First we tried the most direct route on a little road which looked as if it had been gritted and cleared. But it turned out to be just the local farmer who had dug a route out of his farm with his tractor. We ended up in his farmyard, where he was standing in a thick coat over his pyjamas, looking bemused and wondering if we were thieves at this hour in the morning. We hurriedly reversed and decided to go the longer way round, over the highest point in the locality.

Things went smoothly, climbing up and across the county boundary. All the roads were clear. We were elated. We were going to make it, against the odds. Round another corner, we were nearly there ... then catastrophe struck.

FLUMP – we drove straight into a six feet snowdrift. It was a gentle sound when we hit the wall of snow, similar to a gentle flop on to a mattress. It took an hour to dig the car out. By the time we arrived at the depot, in a dishevelled state, all of the schools had closed and the buses were cancelled. We needn't have made the effort.

In the afternoon conditions had slightly improved thanks to the snow blower and gritters clearing a path, though they were still only mediocre at best. But passengers were sympathetic and not expecting buses to run that day. Most schools were closed. Most, except for the high school I was down to cover. A bus was needed to go down to pick a handful of pupils. In a fit of misplaced bravado, I volunteered.

This time I got stuck because I tried to take a short cut. Again it looked like a road which the gritter had been down. With my previous experiences that day, I should have been more cautious. I wasn't. The further I went, the narrower the ploughed track became. It was just wide enough for a bus. Around the corner and over the bridge and – Oh no – the track stopped and disappeared into the farm next to the bridge. The farmer had just cleared his patch and had gone no further. Everybody seemed to know this was the case ... except me.

"What did you ever want to do a thing like that for? No one ever takes this road when it snows!" commented the driver of a passing four-wheel drive and trailer piled with wood, who passed my stricken bus. It was not worth arguing the point as since returning to driving I found that the more excuses I made, the more I was teased, in line with all other drivers. It was fair game and the best policy was to say very little.

The bus had tried manfully to get up the hill, but skidded in the snow and slowly slid sideways into the farmer's silage pit. The farmer was watching my poor performance from the relative comfort of his barn. Shaking his head, he fetched his tractor and hauled me out. This was the second time in a week I had been forced to rely on the services of Farmer Giles. He had been one of the passing motorists who had stopped to help when I was stuck in my last snowdrift. He had been a bus driver himself and understood that bus drivers made mistakes, but from his actions he made it plain that he had never seen one as inherently stupid as me.

Mike the Mechanic and the boss came down to see what damage I had caused, fearing the worst after my pathetic call for help. They were still muttering various insults under their breath.

"Bloody disaster area", seethed the other boss when I returned to the depot. I retired quietly home once more to lick my wounds.

En route, thirty-five minutes later, I stopped for some shopping in my local village.

"Hear you've had a spot of bother," said one of the ladies in the supermarket.

The bush telegraph had obviously been working overtime. The news had travelled at lightning speed, considering I had only travelled twelve miles in such a short space of time and I was staggered that it had got there before I had.

"How on earth do you know about that?" I asked.

"Well it was my little brother who pulled you out!" she replied.

"That's why I like this place," said my neighbour who originally came from County Wicklow but happened to be standing next to me in the queue and had overheard our conversation. "I've lived all over England, but I've never been to anywhere which is like a small piece of Ireland. Everything is done around here similar to Irish ways."

The valley where I lived was one of four valleys in close proximity, situated in the bosom of the Pennine hills and bordering three counties. At times they seemed to merge into each other, partly because the signs on the border, denoting which county you were in, had often been peppered with shotgun pellets, vandalised or had disappeared as a result of being stolen. This made life hard for tourists and anyone from outside the area, who had no idea which county they were in. It was, of course, before the days of satnav and GPS. The four valleys were also interconnected in that many people in one valley were related to some in other valleys. Not that you would find out until there was a funeral when everybody congregated and it became apparent who was related to whom.

When I returned to the bus depot the next morning, I was made to pay for the consequences of my actions in the snow. I was put on to local service work. I was removed from a private hire to the North Northumberland coast and Holy Island, for fear that I might follow the example set by some Spanish tourists, who recently had been splashed across the local papers, for failing to heed warnings of the incoming tide and becoming stranded on the causeway. My punishment was driving school buses for the next few weeks.

I was called Scott, Disaster Area, Tool. The driver who had been following me the first time I got stuck, and had been giving me a lift when he drove the car into the wall of snow, was convinced I had become his nemesis and that I was a jinx. Every time our paths crossed, something bad seemed to happen to him. He thought it had got so bad that he had taken to wearing a crucifix.

On a school run one morning, having met me earlier, he was driving the bus round a corner when, to his horror, two ponies jumped into the middle of the road. He had no time to brake and hit them. The damage to the front of the bus was sizeable. The lights were smashed and the panels severely dented. The ponies survived in rude health, one galloped away and not seen again for months.

This was red rag to the bull for the bosses and the other drivers and there followed months of teasing. The comments came thick and fast.

"Your throat sounds bad. Are you feeling a little HORSE this morning?"

"Is your bus not powerful enough? Were you trying to increase the HORSE power?"

He avoided me at every opportunity.

It was quite an indictment for him to be so rattled as he was no stranger to outlandish events happening in his life. He had once been a mechanic who mended hearses for funeral directors. When the repairs had been completed the mechanics took the vehicle out on a test drive. For a joke one would lie in a coffin and when the car stopped at the traffic lights raised his head and arms out of the wooden box. This was fun until an elderly couple in the next door car looked into the hearse and, as a result of what they saw appeared to have simultaneous heart attacks.

Being confined to driving school buses was not really so bad. The school bus parks were similar to the coach parks in the tourist towns; places where bus drivers congregated and talked about the latest gossip while waiting for the end of school. The current talk was of a driver who was in a bit of trouble. He had a weak bladder and had been forced to stop the bus down a narrow lane because he could not hold on any longer. He jumped down the steps and just made the verge and peed, without a thought of who was watching. Complaints had reached the parents who were about to ring the police, but they calmed down slightly when a medical certificate was produced.

The other topic of discussion was a local school bus which had erupted into open warfare. Some children had fallen out with other children. The parents of those children had fallen out with each other. They had, in turn, fallen out with the teachers, the bus drivers and numerous people at the council.

In between attempting to throttle each other, two children had been seen whacking another passenger over the head with their seatbelts. They had picked on the village drunk, who would be returning from lengthy drinking sessions in the pub and did not seem to notice the discomfort or pain which was being inflicted upon him.

He was no stranger to controversy himself. On the way home, one late night, he uprooted a snow post (placed along hilltop roads to give motorists guidance in the snow) with a view to chopping it up for firewood later. The next morning brought the sad realisation that this would never be possible as it was a concrete post.

The trouble continued. A past, much loved, local bus driver called

Willie would have rolled in his grave at any vandalising behaviour happening on his school bus. It just wouldn't have been tolerated. But those were more genteel days and Willie once stopped on his route during a heavy snowstorm to pick up some passengers. There was a sizeable queue and at the head of the queue was a large lady. A man made the error of barging in front of her to escape the cold. Her angry voice could be heard the length of the bus and she yelled, "Excuse me! Ah's first."

To which Willie replied,

"It does not matter which way round you get on the bus. Just hurry up!"

Another time when Willie pulled into a bus stop, a lady came down the aisle with a breast hanging out of her blouse, and he had said disapprovingly, "Madam, you really should make yourself decent."

She stopped. Thought for a second and said, running back, "Oh my goodness! I've left my baby on the bus."

The end of school was late that day. The chit chat in the bus park went on while we waited for the children to run out. It continued along the theme of quirky bus drivers.

"He's so laid back! In fact, he is in the process of writing a book," said one driver about a colleague who could always be found in the depot drinking cups of tea. "A book about the history of lay-bys."

Then there was the driver who was a little too fussy and genteel in his behaviour. The children nicknamed him Gladys as, in their words, was a 'big girl's blouse.'

"And you see that one over there," said the main storyteller. "Watch the way he walks and carries his head. They call him the Bantam Cock."

The unforgiving nature of describing other drivers was consistent in the industry and I often laughed at the thought of what they were saying about me.

* * * * *

As my driving and the weather improved making the chance of an accident diminish, I was to split my time between the schools and the Vallium Run, the 11-hour shift, subsidised by the council, with very few passengers on board and a wearing day for the drivers. The service ran to and from a tiny village which the bus drivers named, the Land That God Forgot. Peculiar things happened there. The inhabitants were a volatile and vociferous mixture who rarely shied away from lambasting the bus driver for anything which displeased them.

A relatively new 31-seat Mercedes midi bus had been acquired by the company to fulfil the contract. It became known as the 'Flying Pig' by all drivers due to being sluggish, noisy and juddering, or Le Cochon Volant by a passing French tourist. One driver was so unnerved by the rattling noises that he wore ear defenders all day in summer and furry ear muffs in winter. Other drivers moaned about having to do 'Double Valliums' or 'Triple Valliums' each week, as if it was a form of punishment. I found it had its good points and bad, but there was always something unconventional happening each day.

The high spot was the first morning trip up to the coach park of a Roman fort where there was a twenty-minute break and the lady in the shop gave you a free cup of coffee. Regrettably this ceased when the lady left.

The first day I drove the service, I completed the 211 miles (337km) round trip without a hitch. The second day I did not. Driving through the main town was hazardous at the best of times. But from 9am to 5pm the parking verged on anarchic. People parked anywhere, particularly where there were narrow bits and double yellow lines. There was one Community Liaison Officer to sort out this mess, who walked up and down the street, smiling beautifully at everybody, but seemed to lack the authority to do much except smile. Offenders who parked on double yellow lines waved and smiled back as they ran into the shops. On rare occasions, the police made a flying visit from the next town and a dozen cars would be ticketed. The place emptied and turned into a ghost town for a short time. Within the hour everything had returned to normal when the grapevine announced that the squad cars had left the town.

That morning I had overheard a motorist talking to the policeman as he was slapping a ticket on his windscreen. He looked close to tears: "But I only parked here so that my wife could pick up the paper."

"Well sir, it's was a very expensive paper," replied the officer as he handed over the ticket.

I wondered if he was the same policeman who had stopped a friend of my wife as she was leaving another town for speeding in a 30mph limit. "Officer, I cannot possibly have been speeding as I was going uphill," she said innocently. "I could understand it if I was going downhill, like I was earlier. But not uphill."

"Madam," the po-faced rozzer replied as he wrote the summons "please note that the speed restriction applies in both directions – both downhill and uphill."

By mid morning the police raid had finished and I was driving up the high street, having just picked up two passengers at the railway station. I was in the larger 11-metre bus as the Flying Pig had broken down and was being mended back at the depot. Halfway up, I had to stop as there was an illegally parked white van on the pavement, sticking out into the middle of the road with not enough room to get past. There was no sign of the driver. The traffic backed up behind me.

One of the local shopkeepers stepped out into the road and started trying to guide me past using wild arm movements. I should have known better. In the past I have found it best not to follow directions from members of the public as they have no concept of size or distance and it usually ends in tears. The backed up motorists were getting angry so I decided to try.

He waved frantically, gesticulating with a kind of sign language I didn't really understand. The more he waved, the closer the bus came towards the van's wing mirror. I inched past and was doing fine until a thick protruding rubber piece on the emergency exit door at the rear of my bus gently made contact with the mirror casing. The mirror snapped and dropped to the ground smashing into a thousand pieces.

At the same moment he shop owner pulled his hat down and smartly strode back into his shop and the van driver came out of the betting shop to see what the commotion was about.

"You've smashed my mirror," he growled.

To my amazement I didn't have to reply as pedestrians who were walking along the pavement carrying their shopping bags unexpectedly came to my aid as witnesses. More and more ladies seemed to appear out of nowhere, surrounding the 22-stone van driver and jabbing their fingers into his chest saying he was to blame. Another bus driver stopped his bus and helped too. As I got back into my bus and drove off, I was chased by the van driver who was running up the middle of the road straddling the white lines. By the first corner he had run out of puff and had given up the pursuit. In my mirror I could still see my army of witnesses who continued to harangue him. God bless them, I thought, as I drove off.

* * * * *

The regular passengers on the Vallium Run were an eclectic bunch. None more so than the one the drivers nicknamed the Champagne Lady. She would always appear on the bus with her canvas shopping trolley, and ask the driver to carry it on to the bus when returning from the town.

"By heaven, this is heavy," said the driver. "What have you got in there?"

"A big bag of potatoes," she replied with a straight face.

While he carried it on to the bus the top flap came undone, flew open and revealed many bottles of champagne. She then told the truth and said that she loved champagne and when there was an offer at the supermarket, she would stock up.

Machine Gun Lady was also a regular traveller and so named because of her rapid fire speech, without ever drawing breath. She would describe her doctor's visits, pub visits, family visits in great detail and would still be talking when she had to get off the bus. Even the schoolchildren seemed to go into a tranquil state when the Machine Gun Lady when the bus doubled up as a school bus twice a day. The only time I ever saw her stop talking was when a schoolgirl tripped on the bus steps, dislodging the plastic container holding her lunch box, which contained a Mediterranean Pasta Provencale that was projected down the aisle all over the passengers' feet. The whole bus stank of garlic, tomato and basil for days.

* * * * *

I was subjected to more purgatory when I was once again assigned the school sickness runs, transporting children from all over the country to the outward bound centre. As usual, most schools showed a blatant disregard for the helpful advice regarding eating very little and drinking only water to stave off travel sickness. Many teachers scowled when I brought up the subject either in revulsion of the dictatorial driver or in some cases as an insult to their pride.

"You're not going to be like the bus driver we had last year, are you?" the teacher said when I tried to broach the subject. "He must have thought we had fed the children too much and rudely asked, "Are you going for the record?" As he told me this he handed out some chocolate biscuits to his class. I remained tactful and said nothing.

Eight children were sick before the bus had even left the straight of the motorway. At least they were not quite as bad as a school I had taken a week later who insisted on feeding the children doughnuts and chocolate milk shakes. It took less than 500 yards from the school gates they had departed from for something to happen, with the parents were still waving. That day the casualty hit rate edged into double figures and kept mounting.

Naturally I was blamed for the speed at which I drove around the corners.

* * * * *

"Don't worry about locking the bus, lad," was the advice I was greeted with by a cheery school janitor in Hull, "they'll take your wheels anyway."

The teachers had been equally matter-of-fact, when we had turned into the street where the school was and the parked cars on either side of the road made manoeuvring a bus difficult and hazardous with barely inches to spare.

"I don't like the look of this," I told them nervously.

"Well, lad," said the group leader, "you have two choices. Either you have to come down this street from top end or from the bottom end. So I should just get on with it."

Going to schools in Yorkshire was an experience in how not to mince your words. In the era we live in where thanks to the internet the world is becoming smaller by the day, it was refreshing to go to a place which had retained its identity. The people still spoke with the same economy and bluntness as celebrity ambassadors like Geoffrey Boycott.

Work was constant with contracts to and from the outward bound centre. But it was arduous work because of the early starts. The schools needed to be there between 11 and 11.30am, meaning that if they were situated in Leeds, Hull or Manchester the bus could leave no later than 8.30am. But to get down for that time and to have the legally required 45-minute break, I had to leave the depot at 4am. The good thing was there were never any traffic delays. The weather patterns were erratic and variable, often foggy and icy. The heaters on the bus were temperamental. They were too hot in summer and too cold in winter. This had its plus side though, as it often sent the children into a drowsy state.

* * * * *

"What have you broken, now?" said Mike the burly mechanic, as he studied the defect report I had just submitted. I had a reputation for breaking and denting things. This was therefore the phrase the fitter used the most, when he talked to me. The atmosphere in the depot was relaxed and there was often a gaggle of bus drivers discussing the pros and the cons of local residents and passengers on the bus. Vinegar Jugs, Crusty Flaps and The Rottweiler received the standard treatment and were a reliable fallback in the unlikely event that there was nothing else to talk about.

Across the main road the usual household dispute of the couple who lived in the cottages was beginning to develop and hot up. They were renowned for flying off the handle, hitting and screaming at each other on the pavement outside their front door. The noise rose above the sounds of the bus engines warming up and everyone stopped talking and turned to watch.

I broke the silence by trying to answer the mechanic's question "Just the accelerator," I said, "but not my fault – it just stuck." He didn't believe me and like all mechanics he held the firm belief that buses were fine and it was just the drivers who were the problem. Earlier that morning en route to a local beauty spot, the accelerator had jammed at full revs going through some traffic lights and the bus had lurched forward towards some railings. My heart had skipped a beat and I had ceased daydreaming immediately. I thought that maybe this was it and my number was up.

"Oh shit," I said rather too loudly. The teacher sitting behind me flinched uncomfortably, but at least it diverted her attention away from the likelihood that we were about to crash. I managed to bend down and pull the pedal with my hand and steer one handed, just avoiding the bollards and ornate metal railings. "Rude man," I heard her mutter to her colleague sitting next to her. It was no surprise to hear that she had requested another driver the next time she hired a bus.

Of course I was not flavour of the month again with the boss. Coming out of the depot the next morning, the bright sun had temporarily blinded me and I turned the steering wheel too early, driving the side of the bus into the steel frame of the roller door. Luckily I felt it and stopped quickly, flinging the bus into reverse immediately. But the damage had been done and there was still a dent in one of the side panels.

"You're a disaster!" reiterated the boss, struggling for words to describe my actions. "What are you? You are the only driver to have successfully hit the door on all sides. First it was the diesel pump and left hand side of the door with an old Volvo, then you hit the top of the door with the double decker and now you've hit the right side."

* * * * *

I reverted to a more peaceful existence, driving across the moors the next day. It was a Sunday and it was Springtime. This Spring was as glorious as ever. The commute to the depot on that Sunday was as pleasurable as it could be. The moorland was heaving with new life and vitality. Newborn lambs were leaping about all over the place. Grouse flew along the side of the bus at driver's window level. It was as if they are either playing a game or defending their territory. They made a noise which sounded like 'goback, goback, goback', warning all not to trespass on their patch. The pheasants were more aggressive and stupid. They were at their most beautiful with puffed up red cheeks and finely defined markings on their back. Their failings were their small brains and suicidal tendencies to run at a bus and try and attack it in a fit of bravado.

The rabbits were in a blind panic, changing direction and hurling themselves under the wheels of the car. Hares were up on their hind legs boxing each other. Black cocks were conducting their lek and attacking each other. Clouds of peewits (lapwings) were making a beautiful noise and dive bombing anyone who got close to their nest. Curlews floated down from the skies also making their haunting call. Snipe were zigzagging and making a drumming sound with their wings, in their courtship flights. Partridges were scooting up and down the roads chirping. Sometimes there was an adult female woodcock swooping down to carry its chick off to safety in her beak.

I arrived at the depot at 9.30am and enjoyed the emptiness. I was due to pick up some ramblers in one part of the dales and shuttle them 20 minutes down the road to another part of the dales. Being at the depot on a Sunday morning was a different experience from the usual weekday dawn rush as drivers chatted, buses coughed and spurted out acrid diesel smoke. I was the only person around and I revelled in the peace and quiet. The only noise was the incessant chattering of sparrows sitting on the rusting steel beams high up.

Outside the depot, in the heart of the village, nothing stirred.

As I had time to burn, I retired to the primitive drivers' lavatory. It was a basic affair, lacking a seat and the flushing mechanism had not worked for years. One of the older drivers took it on himself to pour a whole bottle of bleach into the bowl occasionally in an attempt to keep it clean. Other drivers topped it up with blue loo chemicals, which were usually reserved for the buses onboard toilets. There was no roof. A piece of Perspex had been placed on top many years ago, but this was so worn that there was a just a gaping hole. It was a very good place to view of the poor state of the metal struts in the roof.

The tranquillity came to an abrupt end with a crash at the other end of the building, which sent me leaping in the air. I went to investigate and found a pane of glass in the roof had broken free and crashed to the ground. This was not a major concern. It happened all the time and it was a miracle that the building had stood for so long, defying many of the laws of physics.

For the next few days I discovered that I was working on the final days of the Newcastle service In the past year there had been murmurs of a radical overhaul of bus routes by the councils. Even though it had been under threat for a long time, it was still a shock and a big loss for the rural community when the news came. It had operated since the 1930s. The atmosphere on the bus was depressed. One pensioner said, "I am very sad because you always knew that if you were in Newcastle without any money, this bus company would get you home."

All the buses had carried a letter, sellotaped to the front window. The gist of the letter was to blame the local politicians for the demise of the service saying:

"Further to the six-month trial period, the council are going to withdraw the subsidy needed to operate this service. We would like to take this opportunity to thank all our customers past and present for their support. Sadly after 80 years of operation the supposed policy of local and Central Government to encourage the use of public transport would appear to be a myth!"

In reality, the local people were mainly to blame for its closure. Over a hundred turned up at a public meeting and told the council they had no right to end the service. Many at that meeting promised they would use it, so the council gave it a six-month trial and promised that the bus would continue after that, subject to a minimum number of passengers. Only a handful used it which was the final nail in the coffin and the funding was therefore removed, meaning that the service had to be pulled. It was the shape of things to come in the bus industry. Cuts were on the way.

* * * * *

Another area which was dwindling was the amount of trips abroad. For many years the company had been engaged by a tour operator to transport schools on skiing trips to France and Italy. In view of my recent imbecility in the snow, I was not allowed anywhere near the Alps. Instead I was given the job of driving the feeder service, picking up the customers at various points and driving them down to Dover. Because of the strict EU regulations on drivers' hours, for any continental trip it was necessary to send the two drivers who were going to drive in Europe in a hire car to a hotel near the port. Then another driver would drive the dull bit from say Glasgow, or Carlisle or Edinburgh to Dover, stay the night in the hotel before heading home in the hire car the next day. That was me.

The first feeder I drove was with a second driver who was meant to show me the ropes. He was a forthright person who said exactly what he felt and had occasional outbursts of temper. While I was waiting at a service station coach park near the port to hand over to the relief drivers I watched as he snapped and picked up an awkward schoolboy by the lapels of his ski jacket and carried him to the side of the bus. He then proceeded to give him an almighty rocket for annoying him by wanting an item from his suitcase which was packed in the bus hold meaning the bus had to be unloaded.

"You should have seen him last week," said the relief driver, "when we were driving through the port and a German in a BMW pulled out in front of him. He didn't like it one bit. He swore blue murder, shook his fist and flashed his lights at the German, calling him a variety of names. He went apoplectic when this German wound down his window and stuck one finger in the air and in a fit of rage he tailgated him, driving a couple of feet away from his bumper. The fundamental Christian group who were sitting behind ended up kneeling on the floor and praying.

Feeders were always long days and it was a welcome sight to see my hotel. All I wanted to do was to collapse on the bed and have a few hours sleep. This was not to be when I was collared by the steely eyed receptionist, who had been having a running battle with the bus company over changing sheets. The other drivers had failed to warn me that she was on the warpath and ready to pounce when I asked what was the innocent request of giving me the key to the room.

"Are you from that northern bus company who booked in yesterday?" she said disapprovingly. "I and my boss are very worried about the number of sheets we have to wash." The miserly attitude was unwarranted considering the bus company was such a good customer and her point blank refusal to change the bed linen every night for different drivers who were coming in was just pedantic. I was too tired to argue and I stomped off to bed. When I found my room, the beds were unmade. The previous drivers had used all the towels and thrown them on the bathroom floor. The rubbish was overflowing in the bin and all the coffee and powdered milk sachets were empty or had disappeared. I did not even bother turning on the television. The walls were so wafer thin that I could hear what the person in the next room was tuned into. I collapsed on the ruffled sheets and blankets, fully clothed and was asleep in under a minute.

That was the last time the company stayed in that hotel. All the drivers were relieved as the place seemed to be a magnet for passionate pigeons. The next morning I was woken by a clamorous ruffling of feathers and looked out of the window to see two mating birds.

* * * * *

The next time I drove a feeder, it was from a northern university. The mixed hockey teams were going on the tortuously long drive down to the Costa Brava, for a week-long sports tournament. This was just an excuse for a week of heavy drinking and excess partying. Every year they had to find a new town who would be prepared to act as hosts as they had been evicted from every other resort for their drunken behaviour. The resort town they were heading for, in Catalonia was either naive or blissfully unaware of the students' reputation.

The students were in an exuberant mood when they joined the bus. They were in such good spirits because many had been up all night and had topped up with an early morning cocktail to keep them going before boarding the bus. Through the haze of drunkenness many of them had packed their passports in their bags. The bags, naturally, had been stowed in the hold.

Unloading all the cases to retrieve the passports gave me something to do while we waited for two students to turn up. Time ticked on and the departure was delayed by one hour. Eventually a taxi appeared and the missing students fell out of the doors, still clutching bottles. They could hardly stand and had to be hauled on to the bus.

Half an hour later, down the motorway, they had sobered up enough to remember that they had left their passports in their bedrooms.

To the surprise of the rest of the group they asked if they could be dropped off at a service station near Wigan, from where they managed to travel under their own steam via a succession of cars, buses, undergrounds and trains arriving at Dover Docks before I did. When the bus rolled in, they were waiting with passports in hand.

The second pick up was at a Midlands university where the ladies netball team boarded the bus. That's when everything livened up. Most of the team under the guidance of their coach and captain hailed from Essex. They were loud and had, like their northern counterparts, been drinking long before the bus arrived. Within ten minutes of setting off, they were singing: 'We are f***ing brill..........all the other teams are w***ers" to the tune of *Nick Nack Paddy Whack, Give The Dog A Bone*. They monopolised the bus CD player and put on music from the 1980s.

Even the heavy partygoers who got on the bus first were outdone by the ladies netball team who continued swigging back cans of cider and made occasional dashes to the rear of the bus lifting their shirts to try and liven up the cowering and stunned northerners.

As we journeyed along the M25 and came down the last hill to the toll booths at the foot of the Dartford Crossing, we passed another bus on the inside lane. Alarm bells rang inside my head when I heard the girls' coach shout, "Ready? Altogether now. One. Two. Three. GO ... OOOOOOOO!"

"No stop! Don't do that!" I yelled. But it was too late.

Nothing would have stopped them. The ensuing whooping, screaming and laughter confirmed that they had done the deed. They had placed their bottoms, close to the windows, taken down their jeans and knickers and mooned at the passengers on the other bus.

The traffic slowed as vehicles queued for the toll booths and it was not long before the other bus had caught up and was matching strides with us. The driver looked over and gave me a very angry, old fashioned look. Then it became apparent why. His passengers were all old aged pensioners and seemed to be gasping for air having had their blood pressure raised substantially. The men looked ill and the women were shocked, perhaps at their spouses desire to keep looking.

"Oh dear, I hope they have health insurance," murmured one of the netball team who was sitting behind me.

* * * * *

I was tired when I returned home. So the prospect of driving the local school bus, the next morning, was not appealing. It was to a school on the outskirts of, what used to be, a lovely little market town, but recently like many other towns had hit hard times and some of the charm had been replaced with crime and aggressiveness. Local youths had eradicated the 'r' and the 'v' at crucial points on the town sign and now it read:

BANGTON

Please d i e carefully

All in all the place was beginning to have an air of 'abandon all hope ye who enter' and the passengers who I carried there on my bus seemed to fit in well to this kind of environment.

"Hello you flatulent old fart," said the precocious thirteen-year-old as a form of greeting. She walked off down the aisle before I could respond and turned her attention to the spiky haired boy sitting in the third row back, and gave him two considerable blows across the head with her school file.

"Wotcha, Leon," she said. Leon couldn't hear her. His arms were covering his ears. She turned instead to the lady courier, knowing full well that she was shockable and said: "What do you call a couple of old age pensioners having sex?" The courier blushed.

"Two old bangers, of course."

Dramatic things always seemed to happen in this town, so it was no surprise to see a car embedded in the main window of a tea rooms in the centre. Two young drivers, reputedly aged thirteen and fifteen had stolen a car and had been joyriding. The damage was so great that scaffolding had to be erected quickly and the road was closed and would remain so for at least six months while repairs were carried out.

The previous day I had met a delivery van through another narrow bit near the town, where there was only room for one vehicle. He had ignored the sign which stated no trucks over 7.5 tons allowed. We were stuck. The truck driver was belligerent and refused to reverse. A Mexican stand-off developed as I was equally stubborn. I knew he would eventually give in when I quoted a dubious aspect of the law bus drivers kept up their sleeves that stated if any fare paying passengers were being carried, it was prohibited to reverse on to a public highway, except when there was either a bus company official or policeman in uniform watching the manoeuvre. No one knew for sure whether this was true or not, but it was most useful when I was driving a school bus and children's safety concerns were added to my spiel. It had the desired effect and other motorists complied either meekly or kicking and screaming. The delivery driver failed to mask his visible hatred of me, as he jumped back into his cab and reversed back to the market place.

A second line of defence for bus drivers, in the unlikely event that the spurious reversing law failed, was to turn the engine off, get the flask and the newspaper out, put your feet on the dashboard and wait. It was normally only a few minutes before the other party realised that they were not going to win against a grouchy old bus driver.

I drove on and out of the town into the countryside. In my pride-induced daydream and smug warm feeling of inner satisfaction, I forgot to stop at one of the points where two schoolchildren got off. I was abruptly brought back to reality by the whole bus shouting in unison, and I stamped on the brakes rather too energetically. As the bus came to a juddering halt several hundred yards beyond where I should have stopped, I heard the THUD, THUD, THUD sound of heavy, out of control footsteps careering down the aisle behind me. The girl who had been trying to rile the courier earlier came flying past me with her arms straightened out in front holding her book bag in a defensive posture, before slamming into the front windscreen, having her nose forcibly pressed up against the glass.

"F**king 'ell, man," she said, trying to straighten his clothes.

I opened the door and reflected that if passengers are rude to bus drivers, there was a high probability that something unpleasant might befall them later in the journey. A bus driver was sometimes similar to cabin crew on an airline, who if riled could always get even by performing a deed such as accidentally dropping a cup of coffee in a passenger's lap. Though the bus world lacked the glamour and fantasy of flying, a driver had plenty of tools available for gentle revenge. The stunned schoolgirl was a case in point. It had the desired effect and she was a little more respectful from that moment.

* * * * *

The bus companies were always scrabbling around for drivers. Even when they had a full complement it only needed one driver to call in sick to throw all the rosters into chaos. Other companies were on the phone most days to ask if there was a spare driver and bus to cover a certain school run. I often did this and I was told to take the most talked about school bus where the children had a fearsome reputation. Many drivers refused to drive it.

"You know, Mr Bus Driver, we have been voted the worst school bus in the whole school," said a boy as he got on to the bus.

But they turned out to be the opposite. They were lively and feisty, constantly pulling the curtains and being noisy, but they also had plenty to say for themselves.

"Wow!" said one boy, "What a lovely bus. The ones we normally have are disgusting – better for transporting cows. Though it was not a bad bus it was touching that he had described it in such lavish terms. It was a very old bus and had started its life at Heathrow Airport transporting air crews to and from their planes. It still had the orange flashing light mounted on the roof.

I drove it the next day, when I returned to my usual school run. The standard of behaviour had descended to an all time low. Increasingly there had been vandalism all the school buses on this route. Drivers had found larger amounts of foam innards of seats scattered on the floors. One day a seat was set fire to and left a singed smell for days.

As I was taking the children back home, on that dark and stormy afternoon, the vision from the interior mirror was poor that it was hard to make out what was going on down the back and all I could see was glimpses of shadowy figures moving around. At the first drop-off point, as the children were getting off, a van pulled up sharply in front of the bus. A furious driver boarded the bus and shouted at me, "It's bloody monstrous. Have you seen the state of the road. The little buggers on your bus have been ripping up their classroom books and throwing the paper out of the skylights. The last two miles are like a landfill site. I've a good mind to tell the headmaster."

The alighting children just shrugged their shoulders and grinned. The van driver jumped into his van and roared off. But another man got on to the bus, went straight to the back and scolded the children, threatening detention and a mass punitive bus cleaning operation on a Saturday morning. He was one of the teachers at the school, who happened to be returning home and driving behind the bus. There was no more trouble for months.

* * * * *

Summer had arrived when I was sent to drive the service bus between Tyneside and the Lake District. It was a beautiful day the first time I drove the route that season. The bus route had been running since before the war and had attracted a loyal but mainly elderly following. This season there was a complication with the introduction of free bus passes for pensioners and the rules which governed what time they could start using them. Each council had different rules which made it all the more confusing. Hence the number of passengers who boarded at the central coach station were limited to a few day trippers and tourists as the departure time was fifteen minutes before the passes were allowed to be used.

As a result fifteen minutes into the journey a large group huddled together were always waiting at a windy bus stop next to a roundabout on the outskirts of the city. In the next town I would sometimes be flagged down by an old man in a cap who waved his walking stick to attract the bus driver's eye. He must have suffered from memory loss because each time he asked me to drive him to the doctor's surgery which was down a side street and in a cul-de-sac.

Times had changed at the end of the route in the Lake District town since I had last visited several years ago. Gone were the relaxed days where I used to park in the coach park behind the bus terminus and walk round the town. As the council had tripled the parking charges the boss told all drivers to go out of the town and find some lay-by to park in for free. It was easier said than done as every other bus company had the same idea and I ended up having to park miles away.

There was nothing to do except lie down on the back seat and have a kip.

* * * * *

The next day I was returning from an early morning school run, when I came around the corner to find the butcher's delivery van stopped in the middle of the road with his hazard lights flashing. The driver was out of his cab and staring at something wriggling in the ditch.

It was a very sick, lost ferret. Quite undeterred he picked up the animal, carried it over to his truck and put it on his jacket on the seat in the cab, where it fell asleep.

"I'm always picking up animals and taking them home with me," he said. "Last week I had a squirrel to stay."

This time he took the ferret in to the local vet where it made a good recovery. The delivery had carried in a box of broken pies

Chapter 9

and asked the nurse if she wanted any for the animals in the hospital. She said she didn't so he carried the trays back on to his van. By chance some of my bus driving colleagues had been standing outside the next door building, having just cleaned out the bus company store when they saw the driver with a basket of pies. They were mortified, thinking that he had been collecting pies which had been made by the vets and they dared not think which dead animals had been used for the filling. They vowed never to go to that butchers shop ever again. It showed how the rumour mill could quickly get out of hand.

* * * * *

The old folks and ladies from the Women's Institute came out of hibernation in the early summer months and I drove them on several day trips. First to Ayr, where I dropped them off in the town centre then parked on the seafront, which was an error as it seemed to be where the alcoholics congregated. It was a cloudless day and I was sitting in the front seat feeling relaxed and admiring the sea view, when a drunk positioned himself on the steps and, uninvited, began discussing the merits of cheap drink and his liking for Buckfast tonic wine or Buckie as he called it. I was divided as to whether I should boot him off my bus, but took the spineless option of sitting and listening to him in case he turned violent.

I have bored people rigid with my view that a bus driver, by nature of visiting so many places and meeting so many people, knows what is going on in the world and has useless pieces of trivia stashed away, so here was my chance to learn more about Scottish drinking habits. I could soon recite most of the nicknames he had used to describe the Buckfast wine which he had an obsession about ... Commotion Lotion, Wreck-the-hoose-juice, Mrs Brown and Bendyerdick Broth amongst others. He only left me in peace only when he said he needed to buy another bottle.

On the return trip home I had to make an emergency stop because some of the old folks had drunk too much. One of the passengers had come came rattling down the bus saying,

"Stop! Driver. I'm not feeling too well." But the rest of the party knew that she'd been drinking too many cups of tea. The lady jumped off and I assumed she would head for the nearby blackberry bushes, yet as soon as she had gone down the steps she crouched down on the pavement by the front wheel and took down her lilac trousers. I turned my head away from the mirror and looked straight ahead at the wind turbines on the summit, but could not fail to hear the conversation going on amongst the passengers behind me.

"Has she been sick yet?" asked from a lady sitting at the rear of the bus.

"No" said the couple down the front who had been pretending not to look in the wing mirror.

"Well what's happening then?"

"It's wind!" said the man, turning his head to the voice down the back and giving an exaggerated theatrical wink, "and let's just say, when you gotta go, you've gotta go!"

The bus descended into giggles and then started a debate on the merit of water tablets and what effect they had on various internal organs. The lady in the lilac trousers sensed something was up when she climbed back on board the bus. She tried to fabricate a story of her predicament, "I'm awfully sorry, it is the first time I've ever felt sick on a bus in 45 years of travelling." This made them laugh more.

I decided now was a good moment to drive off quickly. I deliberately didn't look in the mirror to see what had been deposited on the pavement.

Chapter 9

"That's nothing," said the boss, when I returned to the depot and was explaining that I'd had another bizarre day on the buses. "I damaged an old lady today. I stopped by the bridge and she unfortunately missed her footing and fell down through the grate I had parked by, into the drain. "Are you alright, dear?" I asked as she clambered back up on to the pavement. "Yes, yes, I'm fine," she said, "'but I can't seem to find my false teeth."

* * * * *

Life improved again at the weekend, when I took a club to the races. It was the same club who frightened the bookies on their annual trip to the seaside in Seahouses, many years ago. It had changed since my last visit and the rambling Victorian brick church adjacent to the club had been knocked down and a trendy new contemporary place of worship had been erected. Otherwise it was the much the same. Same people, same decoration, same atmosphere.

There were more double yellow lines around all sides of the club and I had to park the bus on one and take my chance. "Don't worry," said the club secretary, "the wardens are are afraid to come round here. One of our members once got a job as parking warden. He lasted three weeks and got fed up with all the abuse and grief he took from the local community. Now he's a house-husband."

I was also greeted by a less than pleased club member who I recognised as the man who had waved to me as I passed him on the way to the club as he walked up the steep hill. "I wasn't waving, I was trying to flag you down for a lift."

After a couple of pints they were ready to board. We set off before 9am. I had to drive to two different places. Half the group were going to stay in a historic market town, drinking all day in the many pubs. The other half were off to the races, drinking all day in the many bars. The banter at the beginning was happy as the group was full of the joys of spring and fortified by some beer.

I put my blue tinted sunspecs on and instantly a loud voice from the back piped up: "No one told us that the bus was going to be driven by George Michael."

The organiser and his blind friend sat directly behind me.

"He's my best friend, but I have to tell you he's a complete c**t," said the organiser .

"I know," replied the friend, "but you are just jealous, because you know that I am a bigger c**t than you."

We had only been driving for half an hour, when the organiser said in an urgent voice,

"Driver, Driver, piss stop needed." I stopped at the nearest truck stop. All the club members descended the steps and found the nearest hedge or wheel of a truck to pee against. They were watched by the truck drivers who were looking out of the cafe window, eating their breakfast. By the time anyone had spurned into action, it was too late as the group had got back on the bus and we headed for the racecourse.

Most racecourses were bus driver friendly. The drivers were given free entry and occasionally a voucher for free food. But this time I was greeted by a gruff security guard standing by the main gate and looking as if she meant business.

"Where's your work sheet, driver?' she asked gruffly.

"Worksheet?" I replied feebly and timidly, "I don't have a worksheet. My bus company never give them out to drivers."

"No worksheet – no entry," and she pointed to where the row of buses were parked. There was no point in arguing, so I sat in my bus and listened to the commentary which drifted over in waves on the wind.

The club members backed a few winners and some of them came home with a few hundred pounds extra. As they wound their way back to the bus, one of them looked at my feet as he spiralled up the steps and asked what size they were. When I told him they were size 15 he turned to his friend and said in a loud voice, "F***k me, Jim, you'd really know about it if one of those boots gave you a kick up your arse. We'd better behave ourselves on the way home." They did apart from standing in a line for a pee along someone's garden wall.

* * * * *

A new bus had arrived to run alongside the Flying Pig on the Vallium Run. It was a smart Mercedes but had a hair-raising quirk that when the brake was pressed, it would accelerate and without warning leap forward. When I drove it for the first time, it was a frosty morning and when I braked I thought I had hit black ice and was heading towards the ditch. The passengers didn't seem to mind. They had their mind on other things.

There had been a rumpus at one of the cottages in the village. Some of the residents had complained that their lights had started to flicker erratically and had called the electricity company. When they inspected the house they noticed that there was an extra cable feeding into the other house's supply which looked like a case of illegal hacking into another person's supply. They looked in through the windows, saw a number of cannabis plants, anything from 200 to 22,000 according to which person you spoke to. The bus was a hive of excitement.

The police had no idea who owned the house, but they thought that a gang from Asia had been running the factory, remaining mainly invisible to the people who lived in the village.

"My husband met one of them who offered him a joint," said a pensioner as she boarded the bus. "He was pleased as he thought it was a leg of lamb and was shocked when he heard what it really was."

The police damaged the property when they raided it, left all the windows open, bagged up all the peat, left it outside the front door of the house and told the local residents to help themselves if they wanted some for their gardens. The victim who suffered the most was a cat, who used to wander around the drug den and lick the puddles. After the bust she seemed to go cold turkey and refused to leave the house.

It was a strange village. All the drivers had an ambivalent relationship with the place. One particularly gruff driver had told off a child on the school run, who had as a result rang his father and complained. The father was waiting at the bus stop and said to the driver:

"Do you like hospital food?" threatening to beat him up.

"Do you like prison food?" bravely replied the driver, shut the door before waiting for an answer.

I used to set off in the morning in anticipation of who I would meet. The village was seen by some as a dumping ground by the council of problem people. Apart from the drinkk and drugs, mental illness and poverty were often evident, yet it was located in beautiful countryside and to pass through it you would never know there was such deprivation.

I met a man who used to come up on the bus from Tyneside every Friday night looking for a girlfriend. He had pasted lonely hearts adverts on the lampposts in the village saying 'Woman Required' to which he said he had a reasonable success rate.

I met an old man who was pleased when an attractive woman moved in next door. He noticed she had a feminine taste in decor, for as he peered through her front window he saw pink frills and red light bulbs. He also noticed that she seemed to have many smartly dressed men friends who had the newest cars, which would be parked outside the house, but thought nothing of it until he went to the club one night and his friend asked: "So what's it like living next to a prostitute?"

He was shocked and complained to the parish council. It opened up a can of worms with the village being divided over whether she should go or stay. The ones who finally forced her eviction were viewed by the others as jealous types. It was thought that they could not afford her prices.

This pensioner typified the area which was full of deceptive appearances; tranquil on the surface with a hard edge underneath. He travelled on the bus every day and free pass for the twenty-minute journey to the nearest town to collect his newspaper. He would reveal a different side to his gentle character when he talked about his youth and looked misty eyed with sentimental pride of the night he fought some men from another town, by winding up the window of his car, trapping one man's fingers and driving off.

"They were great days," he would say looking longingly out the window.

* * * * *

The great days ended when, the next weekend, another driver had a nasty experience on the same route. Three cars overtook and hemmed in the bus. A youth on the bus pleaded with the driver not to open the door as a dozen men with sticks jumped out of the cars and tried to board the bus. Two other ladies on the bus called the police. The driver didn't panic and drove on. When the police arrived they knew exactly who was involved and what the problem was about. It was the same old problem, a fallout over drugs.

At the same time this was happening, I was having troubles of my own on a school run. A bracket holding the fuel tank in position underneath the chassis had broken, causing it to bump along the road and shower sparks everywhere. I had to stop and as usual it was in the middle of nowhere. I was challenged with the things I always am – cold weather, no heating, grumpy children ringing their mothers, angry mothers threatening to punch my eyes out and a long wait.

I sat down on the verge and considered why I continued to drive buses with all the responsibilities and hassles that befell me, especially as the hours were so long and the wage so low. Was it the variety, eccentricity, eclecticism or camaraderie of the industry? Or was it just a form of self masochism?

Half an hour later I was still contemplating, but I knew I would never leave it.

A view from the driver's seat on a crisp winter's morning following snow.

Puncture by the side of the motorway annoys the passengers.

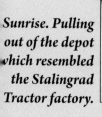

Sunrise. Pulling out of the depot which resembled the Stalingrad Tractor factory.

A history of buses in the North East as seen at an enthusiasts' rally.